Please Leave us a Review on Amazon

Dostoevsky and Christianity

An Interpretation

By
Nikolai Berdyaev

Dostoevsky and Christianity

Translated and edited by
Dean Marais

Published by Based Books
©2026 Dean Marais

Translated into English from the Russian:
First Published in Russian as *Dostoevsky's Worldview* in 1923
By Nikolai Berdyaev (1874-1948)

The cover image is in the public domain
https://commons.wikimedia.org/wiki/File:Dostoevskij_1872.jpg

All rights reserved. No part of this publication may be reproduced, stored in a retrieval system, or transmitted in any form or by any means—electronic, mechanical, photocopying, recording, or otherwise—without the prior written permission of the publisher, except for brief quotations used in reviews, scholarly work, or academic study.

This edition presents a faithful English translation of Nikolai Berdyaev's *Dostoevsky's Wordlview* maintaining the original structure, and style of the 1923 Russian edition for modern readers.

Printed in the United States of America.

Other Works Published by Based Books

The Lives of the Saints for Orthodox Christians – Dean Marais

The New Testament Commentaries of Saint Theophylact of Ohrid

The Complete Discourses of Saint Symeon the New Theolgian

The Sayings of the Desert Fathers: The Patericon of Saint Ignatius Brianchaninov

The Arena - Saint Ignatius Brianchaninov

History of the Byzantine Empire Volumes 1-5 – Dr. Fyodor Uspensky

War, Progress, and the End of History – Vladimir Solovyov

Dostoevsky and Christianity – Nikolai Berdyaev

The Complete Commentaries – Julius Caesar

The Histories Volumes 1-3 – Polybius

The Lives of The Twelve Caesars – Suetonius

The Civil Wars – Appian

The Foreign Wars – Appian

History of the Wars – Procopius

The History of the Church – Eusebius

History of the Roman Empire – Herodian

The Aeneid – Virgil

Geography Volumes 1-2 – Strabo

Getica: The Origins and Deeds of the Goths – Jordanes

Romana: The Origins and Deeds of the Romans - Jordanes

Parallel Lives Volumes 1-5 – Plutarch

Dostoevsky and Christianity

An Interpretation

By
Nikolai Berdyaev

Table of Contents

Preface 11
The Life of Nikolai Berdyaev 12
Chapter I. The Spiritual Image of Dostoevsky 16
Chapter II. Man 29
Chapter III. Freedom 43
Chapter IV. Evil 55
Chapter V. Love 66
Chapter VI. Revolution. Socialism 77
Chapter VII. Russia 90
Chapter VIII. The Grand Inquisitor. The God-Man and the Man-God 105
Chapter IX. Dostoevsky and Us 118

"... Dostoevsky had a defining significance in my spiritual life. Even as a boy I received an inoculation from Dostoevsky. He shook my soul more than any other writer or thinker. I have always divided people into people of Dostoevsky and people foreign to his spirit. The very early orientation of my consciousness toward philosophical questions was bound up with Dostoevsky's 'accursed questions.' Every time I reread Dostoevsky, he revealed himself to me from ever new and different sides. ..."

And the light shines in the darkness, and the darkness has not overcome it. (John 1:5)

Preface

Dostoevsky had a defining significance in my spiritual life. Even as a boy I received an inoculation from Dostoevsky. He shook my soul more than any other writer or thinker. I have always divided people into people of Dostoevsky and people foreign to his spirit. The very early orientation of my consciousness toward philosophical questions was bound up with Dostoevsky's "accursed questions." Every time I reread Dostoevsky, he revealed himself to me from ever new and different sides.

In my youth, the theme of "The Legend of the Grand Inquisitor" lodged itself in my soul with piercing intensity. My first turning to Christ was a turning to the image of Christ in the Legend. The idea of freedom has always been fundamental to my religious world-perception and worldview, and in this primordial intuition of freedom I encountered Dostoevsky as my spiritual homeland.

I have long felt the need to write a book about Dostoevsky, and I realized it only partially in several articles. The seminar on Dostoevsky that I conducted at the "Free Academy of Spiritual Culture" during the winter of 1920–21 finally prompted me to gather all my thoughts about Dostoevsky. And I wrote a book in which I not only attempted to reveal Dostoevsky's worldview, but also invested a great deal of my own worldview.

Moscow, September 23, 1921

The Life of Nikolai Berdyaev

Family

N. A. Berdyaev was born on March 6, 1874, at the Obukhovo estate in Kiev Province. He came from an ancient noble family with traditions of military service. His father, cavalry guard officer Alexander Mikhailovich Berdyaev, served as the marshal of the nobility for the Kiev district and later as chairman of the board of the Kiev Land Bank; his mother, Alina Sergeevna, née Princess Kudasheva, was French on her mother's side. His elder brother Sergei was a poet, publicist, and publisher.

Education

Berdyaev was educated at home, then at the Kiev Cadet Corps. In 1894 he enrolled in the natural sciences faculty of Kiev University, transferring a year later to the law faculty. At university he became captivated by Marxism. In 1897 he was arrested for participating in a student demonstration; the following year he was arrested a second time for possessing and distributing illegal literature and was expelled from the university. In 1900 he was exiled to Vologda, where he remained for two years, and then to Zhitomir.

Public and Political Activity

In 1903–1904 he participated in the creation and activities of the "Union of Liberation,"[1] but felt out of place there.

In 1904 Berdyaev met his future wife, L. Yu. Trusheva; friendly relations were established with L. I. Shestov and S. N. Bulgakov. He became acquainted with D. S. Merezhkovsky, Andrei Bely, V. V. Rozanov, Z. N. Gippius, and Vyacheslav I. Ivanov; he immersed himself "in the very intense and concentrated atmosphere of the Russian cultural renaissance of the early twentieth century" with its literary and artistic achievements and dangerous spiritual temptations.

Berdyaev welcomed the Revolution of 1905, but found disagreeable "the character it assumed and its moral consequences."

In 1907 Berdyaev participated in organizing the Religious-Philosophical Society in St. Petersburg.

In the autumn of 1908 Berdyaev moved to Moscow, where he became acquainted with M. A. Novoselov and participants in his "Circle of Those Seeking Christian Enlightenment." A period of closest proximity to Christianity and the Church began in Berdyaev's life.

In 1911 Nikolai Alexandrovich departed for Italy, where he wrote certain chapters of the book *The Meaning of the Creative Act*, completed in 1914—his first attempt at a systematic exposition of the philosophy of personalism.

Although Berdyaev did not share the ideas of Name-Glorifying[2] and perhaps never delved into them at all, in 1913 he published an article "Extinguishers of the Spirit" in the newspaper *Russkaya Molva* with furious criticism of the Holy Synod's actions to eradicate this error; he was brought to trial, which was postponed due to the outbreak of the World War.

Revolution. Forced Emigration

He greeted the February Revolution with enthusiasm. However, even before the October coup of 1917, disillusionment began; while still condemning the old government and autocracy, Berdyaev became disappointed in the new one, noticing everywhere signs of the destruction of the foundations of life and culture.

In October 1917, for a brief period, Berdyaev became a member of the Council of the Republic representing public figures; in 1918 he became vice-chairman of the All-Russian Union of Writers. In 1919 he founded the Free Academy of Spiritual Culture, which operated until 1922; the most prominent representatives of Russian philosophy were invited to work in it. Berdyaev himself delivered a number of courses—for example, on the metaphysics of history and on the philosophy of Dostoevsky. In 1920 Berdyaev was elected professor at Moscow University. He was arrested twice.

After his expulsion from Russia on September 29, 1922—on the so-called "philosophers' steamship," having been made to sign an acknowledgment that if he attempted to return to the country he would be shot at the border—Berdyaev lived first in Berlin, then in Paris. He founded the Religious-Philosophical Academy and the journal *Put'* [The Way] associated with it (published from 1925 to 1940, with 61 issues released). In his article "The Living Church and the Religious Rebirth of Russia" he sharply condemned the "Living Church" movement.

It is noteworthy that the academy was opened with the support of John R. Mott, a prominent figure in Protestantism, an ecumenist, and one of the founders of the World Council of Churches. The journal *Put'* was printed by the well-known YMCA-Press publishing house.[3]

In 1924 Berdyaev became one of the founders of the "Orthodox Brotherhood in the Name of Holy Sophia, the Wisdom of God." Two years later he withdrew from the brotherhood and participated in its meetings only as a guest. He explained his departure by citing political disagreements with P. B. Struve and the absence of genuine churchly brotherhood.

Attitude Toward Christianity

N. A. Berdyaev actively participated in the Russian Student Christian Movement (RSCM), was one of its ideologists, a zealous advocate of Christian unity, and a participant in ecumenical conferences.

In Christianity Berdyaev saw the true religion uniting God-Christ with man. However, he considered the restoration of patristic Christianity dangerous (*The Meaning of the Creative Act*, ch. II). He accepted the Kabbalistic teaching about the "heavenly Adam" and spoke of the similarity of all religions in the idea of overcoming the world.

Berdyaev's understanding of Christianity took shape within the current of "new religious consciousness"—a religious-philosophical movement of that part of the Russian intelligentsia which, finding itself outside the Church, sought its own path to God. Berdyaev was greatly captivated by the pathos of "God-seeking." The main features of the "new religious consciousness"—rejection of "scholastic theology," criticism of the Church and historical Christianity, an inclination toward gnostic mysticism as directly uniting the person with God, belief in a new syncretic religion of Christianity which, alongside the distinctive features of existing Christian churches, would assume new forms of consciousness and culture—left a deep mark on Berdyaev's worldview. He became a convinced advocate of reinterpreting the fundamental theological and religious concepts of Christianity.

Here are examples of non-Christian, non-churchly statements by N. A. Berdyaev. He writes that recognition of hierarchical authority in the Church passes over into idolatry. This position is close to the Protestant one, which denies hierarchy. Berdyaev promoted ideas of social evolution, asserting that "in Christianity's past, integral spirituality had not yet been revealed... because the problem of human labor, which connects man with cosmic life, had not been spiritually resolved" (*Spirit and Reality*). That is, it turns out that in Christ spirituality was not revealed. Berdyaev considers that "a fateful role in the history of Christian spirituality was played by the idea of obedience. Obedience is false spirituality. It inevitably degenerates into obedience to evil and engenders slavery" (*Spirit and Reality*). This thought completely contradicts the Orthodox teaching on obedience.

The conception of a "philosophy of Christianity" arose in Berdyaev early: already in 1905, in the article "On the New Religious Consciousness," he wrote about the necessity of uniting religious experience with contemporary philosophy in order to overcome what he considered the limitations of "theological schools."

Berdyaev interpreted Sacred Tradition as broadly as possible, including in it philosophical, gnostic, mystical, and other teachings about God; thus, for him the bearer of Tradition was not only the Church but also culture.

Final Years

About his final years of life he writes: "In recent years a small change occurred in our material situation; I received an inheritance, though a modest one, and became the owner of a pavilion with a garden in Clamart. For the first time in my life, already in exile, I had property and lived in my own house, although I continued to be in need—there was never enough."

In Clamart, "Sundays" with tea were held once a week, at which Berdyaev's friends and admirers gathered; conversations and discussions of various questions took place, and "one could speak about everything, express the most opposing opinions."

In 1947 Berdyaev was elected an honorary doctor of Cambridge University. His books *The Russian Idea* and *Essay in Eschatological Metaphysics* were published.

Berdyaev continued writing until the final minutes of his life; death found him at his writing desk.

Nikolai Alexandrovich Berdyaev died on March 24, 1948, in Clamart and was buried there. The funeral service was performed by Archimandrite Nikolai (Yeryomin), rector of the Three Hierarchs Metochion, which is under the jurisdiction of the Moscow Patriarchate.

Endnotes:

[1] "Union of Liberation"—an illegal political movement for the introduction of political freedoms in Russia. The founding congress was held in Switzerland in 1903. The movement's program aimed at replacing autocracy with a constitutional monarchy, the right of nationalities to self-determination, compulsory alienation of privately owned lands, and other goals.

[2] Name-Glorifying (*Imyaslavie*), Name-Worship (*Imyabozhnichestvo*)—a religious movement that arose among simple monks in Russian monasteries on Mount Athos in 1909–1913 and found supporters in Russia. The Name-Glorifiers held that God is wholly present in the Divine Name, that the Name of God is God Himself. The teaching of Name-Glorifying was condemned as heretical by the Holy Synod of the Constantinople Orthodox Church and the Holy Synod of the Russian Orthodox Church (1913).

[3] YMCA (Young Men's Christian Association)—a non-confessional youth organization that arose in the nineteenth century with the aim of introducing non-confessional ecumenical ideology among Christian youth. To carry out its activities, it makes use of financial and political support from Freemasonry, widely propagating its principles: 1) the equal value of all confessions; 2) denial of the Divine nature of the Savior and declaration of Him as an ordinary man; 3) unification of all religions into one; 4) realization of the "Kingdom of God" on earth in a distorted, non-Christian sense—that is, in effect, the establishment of the kingdom of the Antichrist.

Chapter I.
The Spiritual Image of Dostoevsky

I do not intend to write a historical-literary study of Dostoevsky, nor do I propose to give his biography and a characterization of his personality. Least of all will my book be an essay in the field of "literary criticism"—a genre of creative work that I do not value highly. Nor would it be accurate to say that I approach Dostoevsky from a psychological point of view, that I am uncovering Dostoevsky's "psychology." My task is different. My work belongs to the realm of pneumatology, not psychology. I wish to reveal the spirit of Dostoevsky, to bring forth his deepest world-perception, and to intuitively recreate his worldview.

Dostoevsky was not only a great artist; he was also a great thinker and a great seer of the spirit. He is a genius of dialectic, the greatest Russian metaphysician. Ideas play an enormous, central role in Dostoevsky's creative work. His brilliant dialectic of ideas occupies no less a place in Dostoevsky than does his extraordinary psychology. This dialectic of ideas is a special form of his artistry. Through his art he penetrates into the very foundations of the life of ideas, and the life of ideas permeates his art. In his work, ideas live an organic life; they possess their own inescapable, vital destiny.

This life of ideas is a dynamic life; in it there is nothing static, no stagnation and no ossification. Dostoevsky investigates the dynamic processes in the life of ideas. In his creative work, a fiery whirlwind of ideas rises up. The life of ideas unfolds in an incandescent, fiery atmosphere—cooled ideas do not exist in Dostoevsky, and he takes no interest in them. Truly, there is something of the Heraclitean spirit in Dostoevsky. Everything in him is fiery and dynamic, everything in motion, in contradictions and struggle. For Dostoevsky, ideas are not frozen, static categories—they are fiery currents.

All of Dostoevsky's ideas are bound up with the fate of man, with the fate of the world, with the fate of God. Ideas determine destiny. Dostoevsky's ideas are profoundly ontological, rooted in being, energetic, and dynamic. Within an idea is concentrated and concealed the destructive energy of dynamite. Dostoevsky shows how the explosions of ideas destroy and bring ruin. Yet within an idea is also concentrated and concealed the energy that resurrects and regenerates.

Dostoevsky's world of ideas is utterly distinctive, unprecedented in its originality, and quite unlike the world of ideas of Plato. Dostoevsky's ideas are not prototypes of being, not primary essences, and certainly not norms; they are destinies of being, primordial fiery energies. Yet no less than Plato did he recognize the determining significance of ideas. Contrary to the modernist fashion that tends to deny the independent significance of ideas and to suspect their value in every writer, one cannot approach Dostoevsky, one cannot understand him, without delving deeply into his rich and distinctive world of ideas.

Dostoevsky's creative work is a veritable feast of thought. Those who refuse to partake in this feast—on the grounds that in their skeptical reflection they have come to suspect the value of all thought and every idea—condemn themselves to a dreary, impoverished, and half-starved existence. Dostoevsky opens up new worlds. These worlds exist in a state of turbulent movement. Through these worlds and their movement, the fates of humanity are deciphered.

But those who limit themselves to an interest in psychology, to the formal aspects of artistry—they close off their own access to these worlds and will never understand what is revealed in Dostoevsky's creative work. And so I wish to enter into the very depths of Dostoevsky's world of ideas, to comprehend his worldview. What is a writer's worldview? It is his contemplation of the world, his intuitive penetration into the inner essence of the world. It is that which is revealed to the creator about the world, about life. Dostoevsky had his own revelation, and I wish to comprehend it.

Dostoevsky's worldview was not an abstract system of ideas; such a system cannot be sought in an artist, and indeed it is hardly possible at all. Dostoevsky's worldview is his brilliant intuition of human and cosmic destiny. This intuition is artistic, but not merely artistic—it is also an ideational, cognitive, philosophical intuition; it is gnosis. Dostoevsky was, in a certain special sense, a gnostic. His creative work is knowledge, a science of the spirit. Dostoevsky's worldview is, above all, dynamic in the highest degree, and it is in this dynamism that I wish to reveal it. From this dynamic standpoint, there are no contradictions whatsoever in Dostoevsky. He realizes the principle of coincidentia oppositorum. From a deep reading of Dostoevsky, everyone should emerge enriched with knowledge. And it is this knowledge that I would like to restore in its fullness.

Much has been written about Dostoevsky. Much that is interesting and true has been said about him. Yet there has not been a sufficiently holistic approach to him. Dostoevsky has been approached from various "points of view," judged before the tribunal of different worldviews, and depending on this, different aspects of Dostoevsky have been revealed or concealed.

For some, he was above all an advocate for the "humiliated and insulted"; for others, a "cruel talent"; for still others, a prophet of a new Christianity; for some, he discovered the "underground man"; and for others, he was first and foremost a true Orthodox Christian and herald of the Russian messianic idea. But in all these approaches, which revealed something in Dostoevsky, there was no congeniality with his integral spirit.

For a long time, Dostoevsky remained closed to traditional Russian criticism, as did all the greatest phenomena of Russian literature. N. Mikhailovsky was organically incapable of understanding Dostoevsky. Understanding Dostoevsky requires a particular disposition of soul. To know Dostoevsky, there must be in the knower a kinship with the subject, with Dostoevsky himself, something of his spirit.

Only at the beginning of the twentieth century did a spiritual and intellectual movement begin among us in which souls more kindred to Dostoevsky were born. Interest in Dostoevsky grew extraordinarily among us. Merezhkovsky nevertheless wrote best of all about Dostoevsky in his book "L. Tolstoy and Dostoevsky." But even he was too preoccupied with advancing his entire religious scheme, with the parallel to L. Tolstoy. For him, Dostoevsky often serves merely as a means for preaching the religion of the resurrected flesh, and he does not see the singular distinctiveness of Dostoevsky's spirit. Yet Merezhkovsky was the first to succeed in revealing something in Dostoevsky that had previously remained completely closed. His approach to Dostoevsky is, nevertheless, fundamentally mistaken. Every great writer, as a great manifestation of spirit, must be received as an integral manifestation of spirit. One must intuitively penetrate into the integral manifestation of spirit, contemplate it as a living organism, immerse oneself in it. This is the only true method. One cannot subject a great, organic manifestation of spirit to vivisection; it dies under the surgeon's knife, and contemplating its wholeness becomes impossible. One must approach a great manifestation of spirit with a believing soul, not decompose it with suspicion and skepticism. Meanwhile, people of our epoch are very inclined to operate on any great writer, suspecting in him cancer or some other hidden disease. And the integral spiritual image vanishes; contemplation becomes impossible. Contemplation is incompatible with the decomposition of its object. And so I wish to attempt to approach Dostoevsky by way of a believing, integral, intuitive immersion in the world of his dynamic ideas, to penetrate into the secret recesses of his primordial worldview.

If every genius is national rather than international, and expresses the universal-human through the national, then this is especially true of Dostoevsky. He is characteristically Russian, a Russian genius to the depths, the most Russian of our great writers, and at the same time the most universal-human in his significance and in his themes. He was a Russian man. "I have always been truly Russian," he writes of himself to A. Maikov. Dostoevsky's creative work is a Russian word about the universal-human. And for this reason, of all Russian writers, he is most interesting to Western European people. They seek in him revelations about that universal which torments them as well, but revelations from another world—the enigmatic world of the Russian East. To understand Dostoevsky to the end means to understand something very essential in the structure of the Russian soul; it means to draw near to the unraveling of Russia's mystery. But, as another great Russian genius says:

Russia cannot be grasped by the mind, Nor measured by a common measure.

Dostoevsky reflects all the contradictions of the Russian spirit, all its antinomian character, which admits the possibility of the most contradictory judgments about Russia and the Russian people. Through Dostoevsky one can study our distinctive spiritual structure. Russian people, when they most fully express the distinctive traits of their nation, are either apocalypticists or nihilists. This means that they cannot remain in the middle of the soul's life, in the middle of culture; their spirit is directed toward the final and the ultimate. These are two poles, positive and negative, expressing one and the same striving toward the end. And how profoundly different is the structure of the Russian spirit from that of the German—Germans are either mystics or critics—and from that of the French—the French are either dogmatists or skeptics. The Russian psychic constitution is the most difficult for the creation of culture, for the historical path of a people. A people with such a soul can hardly be happy in its history. Apocalypticism and nihilism, from opposite ends—the religious and the atheistic—equally overthrow culture and history as the middle of the path. And it is often difficult to determine why a Russian declares rebellion against culture and history and overthrows all values, why he strips himself bare—is it because he is a nihilist, or because he is an apocalypticist striving toward the all-resolving religious end of history?

In his notebook Dostoevsky writes: "Nihilism appeared among us because we are all nihilists." And Dostoevsky investigates Russian nihilism to its depths. The antinomian polarity of the Russian soul combines nihilism with a religious striving toward the end of the world, toward a new revelation, a new earth and a new heaven. Russian nihilism is a perverted Russian apocalypticism. Such a spiritual disposition greatly impedes the historical work of a people, the creation of cultural values; it is very unfavorable to any discipline of the soul. This is what K. Leontiev had in mind when he said that a Russian can be a saint but cannot be honest. Honesty is a moral middle ground, a bourgeois virtue; it holds no interest for apocalypticists and nihilists. And this trait has proved fateful for the Russian people, because only a few elect become saints, while the majority is consigned to dishonesty. Only a few attain the highest spiritual life, while the majority finds itself below the level of average cultural life. This is why in Russia the contrast is so striking between the very small upper cultural stratum of genuinely spiritual people and the enormous uncultured mass. In Russia there is no cultural milieu, no cultural middle, and almost no cultural tradition. In relation to culture, almost all Russians are nihilists. Culture, after all, does not resolve the problem of the end, of the exit from the world process; it consolidates the middle.

To Russian boys (Dostoevsky's favorite expression), absorbed in the resolution of ultimate world questions—whether about God and immortality, or about the ordering of humanity according to a new plan—to atheists, socialists, and anarchists, culture appears as an obstacle in their headlong movement toward the end. Russians counterpose the leap toward the end to the historical and cultural labor of European peoples. Hence the hostility toward form, toward the formal principle in law, the state, morality, art, philosophy, and religion. The formalism of European culture is repugnant to the Russian character; it is alien to him. The Russian has little formal giftedness. Form introduces measure; it restrains, sets boundaries, strengthens one in the middle. Apocalyptic and nihilistic revolt sweeps away all forms, shifts all boundaries, casts off all restraints.

Spengler, in his recently published book *Preußentum und Sozialismus*, says that Russia is an entirely special world, mysterious and incomprehensible to European man, and he discerns in it an "apocalyptic revolt against personality." Russian apocalypticists and nihilists dwell on the outskirts of the soul; they go beyond the limits. Dostoevsky investigated to the depths the apocalypticism and nihilism of the Russian spirit. He discovered a kind of metaphysical history of the Russian soul, its exceptional propensity for possession and demonic frenzy. He investigated to the depths Russian revolutionism, with which Russian "Black Hundredism" is closely connected. And Russia's historical fate has vindicated Dostoevsky's insights. The Russian Revolution took place in significant measure according to Dostoevsky. And however destructive and ruinous it may seem for Russia, it must nonetheless be recognized as Russian and national. Self-destruction and self-immolation are Russian national traits.

This structure of our national soul helped Dostoevsky deepen the psychic into the spiritual, to go beyond the middle ground of the psychic life and to open up spiritual vistas, spiritual depths. Beyond the strata of psychic formation, beyond the settled psychic structure, beyond the psychic layers illuminated by rational light and subordinated to rational norms, Dostoevsky reveals a volcanic nature. In Dostoevsky's creative work, an eruption of subterranean, subsoil volcanoes of the human spirit takes place. It was as if revolutionary spiritual energy had been accumulating for a long time, the soil becoming ever more volcanic, while on the surface, in planar existence, the soul remained statically stable, kept within boundaries, subordinated to norms. And then, at last, a violent breakthrough occurred, an explosion of dynamite. Dostoevsky was the herald of this unfolding revolution of the spirit. His creative work expresses the turbulent and passionate dynamism of human nature. Man tears himself away from every settled way of life, ceases to lead an existence under the law, and passes into another dimension of being.

With Dostoevsky, a new soul is born into the world, a new world-perception. Dostoevsky sensed within himself this volcanic nature, this exceptional dynamism of spirit, this fiery movement of spirit. Of himself he writes to A. Maikov: "But worst of all is that my nature is base and far too passionate: everywhere and in everything I go to the uttermost limit; all my life I have crossed the line." He was a man scorched, consumed by an inner spiritual passion; his soul was in flames. And from the hellish flames his soul ascends toward the light. All of Dostoevsky's heroes are himself, his own path, the various sides of his being, his torments, his questionings, his suffering experience. And therefore in his creative work there is nothing epic, no depiction of objective daily life, no objective structure of life, no gift for reincarnation into the natural diversity of the human world—none of that which constitutes the strong side of Leo Tolstoy. Dostoevsky's novels are not true novels; they are tragedies, but tragedies of a special kind. This is the inner tragedy of a single human fate, a single human spirit, revealing itself only from different sides at different moments of its path.

Dostoevsky was granted the ability to know man in passionate, turbulent, frenzied movement, in exceptional dynamism. There is nothing static in Dostoevsky. He is entirely within the fiery dynamics of spirit, within the fiery element, within frenzied passion. Everything in Dostoevsky occurs in a fiery whirlwind; everything whirls in this vortex. And when we read Dostoevsky, we feel ourselves entirely swept up in this whirlwind. Dostoevsky is an artist of the subterranean movement of the spirit. In this turbulent movement everything is displaced from its usual place, and therefore his art is directed not toward the settled past, like Tolstoy's art, but toward the unknown future. This is prophetic art. He reveals human nature, investigates it not in its stable middle ground, not in its settled, everyday life, not in the normal and normalized forms of its existence, but in the subconscious, in madness and crime. In madness rather than in health, in crime rather than in lawfulness, in the subconscious, nocturnal element rather than in the daylight of ordinary life, not in the light of a consciously organized soul—here the depths of human nature are revealed, its limits and boundaries explored.

Dostoevsky's creative work is Dionysian creative work. He is entirely immersed in the Dionysian element, and this Dionysianism gives birth to tragedy. He draws us into the fiery atmosphere of Dionysian whirlwinds. He knows only ecstatic human nature. And after Dostoevsky, everything seems beautiful. It is as if we had visited other worlds, other dimensions, and returned to our measured, limited world, to our three-dimensional space. A deep reading of Dostoevsky is always an event in one's life; it scorches, and the soul receives a new baptism by fire. A person who has been initiated into the world of Dostoevsky becomes a new person; other dimensions of being are revealed to him. Dostoevsky is a great revolutionary of the spirit. He is entirely directed against the ossification of spirit.

The contrast between Dostoevsky and L. Tolstoy is striking. Dostoevsky was the herald of the unfolding revolution of the spirit; he is entirely within the fiery dynamics of spirit, entirely turned toward the future. And yet he declared himself a man of the soil; he cherished the connection with historical traditions, guarded historical sanctities, acknowledged the historical Church and the historical state. Tolstoy was never a revolutionary of the spirit; he is an artist of statically settled daily life, turned toward the past rather than the future; there is nothing prophetic in him. And yet he rebels against all historical traditions and historical sanctities, denies the historical Church and the historical state with unprecedented radicalism, and refuses any continuity of culture.

Dostoevsky exposes the inner nature of Russian nihilism. Tolstoy himself turns out to be a nihilist, a destroyer of sanctities and values. Dostoevsky knows about the revolution taking place, which always begins in the spiritual subsoil. He foresees its paths and its fruits. Tolstoy does not know that a revolution has begun in the spiritual subsoil and foresees nothing, yet he himself is seized by one aspect of this revolutionary process, like a blind man. Dostoevsky dwells in the spiritual and learns everything from there. Tolstoy dwells in the psychic-corporeal and therefore cannot know what is happening in the very depths; he does not foresee the consequences of the revolutionary process.

Tolstoy's artistry may be more perfect than Dostoevsky's; his novels are the finest in the world. He is a great artist of what has become. Dostoevsky, however, is turned toward what is becoming. The art of becoming cannot be as perfect as the art of what has become. Dostoevsky is a more powerful thinker than Tolstoy; he knows more; he knows opposites. Tolstoy cannot turn his head; he looks straight ahead along a single line. Dostoevsky perceives life from within the human spirit. Tolstoy perceives life from within the soul of nature.

Therefore Dostoevsky sees the revolution taking place in the depths of the human spirit. Tolstoy, however, sees above all the stable, natural order of human life, its vegetative-animal processes. Dostoevsky bases his foresight on his knowledge of the human spirit. Tolstoy straightforwardly rebels against that vegetative-animal human life which is all he sees. And for Dostoevsky, Tolstoy's moralistic straightforwardness proves to be impossible.

Tolstoy, with inimitable perfection, gives artistic comeliness to the established forms of life. For Dostoevsky, as an artist of what is becoming, this artistic comeliness proves unattainable. Tolstoy's art is Apollonian art. Dostoevsky's art is Dionysian art. And in one more respect the relationship between Tolstoy and Dostoevsky is remarkable. Tolstoy spent his whole life seeking God, as a pagan seeks Him, as a natural man distant from God in his very essence. His thought was occupied with theology, and he was a very poor theologian. What torments Dostoevsky is not so much the theme of God as the theme of man and his fate; what torments him is the riddle of the human spirit. His thought is occupied with anthropology, not theology. He resolves the theme of God not as a pagan, not as a natural man, but as a Christian, as a spiritual man resolving the theme of man.

Truly, the question of God is a human question. But the question of man is a divine question, and perhaps the mystery of God is better revealed through the human mystery than through a natural turning to God apart from man. Dostoevsky is not a theologian, but he was closer to the living God than Tolstoy. God is revealed to him in the fate of man. Perhaps one ought to be less of a theologian and more of an anthropologist.

Was Dostoevsky a realist? Before deciding this question, one must know whether great and genuine art can be realistic at all. Dostoevsky himself sometimes liked to call himself a realist and considered his realism to be the realism of actual life. Of course, he was never a realist in the sense that our traditional criticism affirmed the existence of a realistic school of Gogol among us. Such realism does not exist at all; least of all was Gogol such a realist, and Dostoevsky certainly was not one either.

All genuine art is symbolic—it is a bridge between two worlds; it signifies a deeper reality, which is authentic reality. This real actuality can be artistically expressed only in symbols; it cannot be directly and immediately presented in art. Art never reflects empirical reality; it always penetrates into another world, yet this other world is accessible to art only through symbolic representation.

Dostoevsky's art is entirely about the deepest spiritual reality, about metaphysical actuality; it is least of all occupied with empirical everyday life. The construction of Dostoevsky's novels least of all resembles the so-called "realistic" novel. Through the external plot, reminiscent of implausible crime novels, another reality shines through. What is real in Dostoevsky is not the reality of empirical, external everyday existence, not the reality of life's routine, not the reality of rooted social types. What is real in him is the spiritual depth of the human being, real is the fate of the human spirit. Real is the relationship between man and God, between man and the devil; real in him are the ideas by which a person lives.

Those divisions of the human spirit that constitute the deepest theme of Dostoevsky's novels do not lend themselves to realistic treatment. The staggeringly brilliant depiction of the relationship between Ivan Karamazov and Smerdyakov, through which two "I's" of Ivan himself are revealed, cannot be called "realistic." And still less realistic is the relationship between Ivan and the devil. Dostoevsky cannot be called a realist even in the sense of psychological realism. He is not a psychologist—he is a pneumatologist and a metaphysician-symbolist.

Behind the life of consciousness in his work there is always hidden the life of the subconscious, and prophetic premonitions are bound up with it. People are connected not only by those relationships and bonds that are visible in the daylight of consciousness. There exist more mysterious relationships and bonds that descend into the depths of subconscious life. In Dostoevsky, another world always intrudes upon the relationships of people in this world. A mysterious connection binds Myshkin with Nastasya Filippovna and Rogozhin, Raskolnikov with Svidrigailov, Ivan Karamazov with Smerdyakov, Stavrogin with the Lame Woman and Shatov. In Dostoevsky, everyone is fettered to one another by bonds not of this world. There are no chance encounters and no chance relationships in his work. Everything is determined in another world; everything has a higher meaning.

In Dostoevsky there are none of the accidents of empirical realism. All his encounters are as if otherworldly encounters, fateful in their significance. All the complex collisions and interrelations of people reveal not an objectively material, "real" actuality, but the inner life, the inner fate of people. In these collisions and interrelations of people, the riddle of man is resolved, his path is revealed, a cosmic "idea" is expressed. All this bears little resemblance to the so-called "realistic" novel. If Dostoevsky can be called a realist at all, then he is a mystical realist.

Literary historians and critics, who love to uncover all manner of influences and borrowings, like to point to various influences on Dostoevsky, especially in the first period of his work. They speak of the influence of Victor Hugo, George Sand, Dickens, and partly Hoffmann. But Dostoevsky has a genuine kinship with only one of the greatest Western writers—Balzac, who was just as little a "realist" as Dostoevsky. Among the great Russian writers, Dostoevsky is most directly connected to Gogol, especially in his early stories. But Dostoevsky's relation to the human being is essentially different from Gogol's. Gogol perceives the human image as decomposed; in him there are no people—instead of people there are strange mugs and snouts. In this respect, Andrei Bely's art is close to Gogol. Dostoevsky, however, perceived the human image as whole; he discovered it even in the most degraded and fallen. When Dostoevsky reached his full stature and spoke his creative new word, he was already beyond all influences and borrowings—he is a unique, unprecedented creative phenomenon in the world.

Notes from Underground divides Dostoevsky's creative work into two periods. Before *Notes from Underground*, Dostoevsky was still a psychologist, though with a distinctive psychology; he was a humanist, full of compassion for "poor folk," for the "humiliated and insulted," for the heroes of the "dead house." With *Notes from Underground* begins Dostoevsky's brilliant dialectic of ideas. He is no longer merely a psychologist; he is a metaphysician; he investigates the tragedy of the human spirit to its very depths. He is no longer a humanist in the old sense of the word; he now has little in common with George Sand, Victor Hugo, Dickens, and the like. He has definitively broken with the humanism of Belinsky. If he is still a humanist, his humanism is entirely new—tragic.

The human being becomes even more central to his creative work, and human destiny is the exclusive object of his interest. But man is taken not in the flat dimension of humanism, but in the dimension of depth, in a newly revealed spiritual world. Now for the first time that human realm opens which is called "Dostoevskyism." Dostoevsky definitively becomes a tragic writer. In him the anguished quality of Russian literature reaches its highest point of intensity. The pain over the suffering fate of man and the fate of the world reaches white heat.

We never had the Renaissance spirit or Renaissance creativity. We did not know the joy of our own rebirth. Such is our bitter fate. At the beginning of the nineteenth century, in the era of Alexander I—perhaps the most cultured in all our history—something resembling a renaissance flashed for a moment; the intoxicating joy of overflowing creativity was manifested in Russian poetry. Such was the radiant, superabundant creativity of Pushkin. But this joy of creative abundance quickly faded; in Pushkin himself it was poisoned. The great Russian literature of the nineteenth century was not a continuation of Pushkin's creative path—it is all in torment and suffering, in pain over the world's salvation; in it there seems to be an expiation of some guilt.

The mournful, tragic figure of Chaadaev stands at the very threshold of the movement of mature Russian thought in the nineteenth century. Lermontov, Gogol, Tyutchev do not create in the creative superabundance of the Renaissance spirit; they create in torment and pain; there is no effervescent play of forces in them. Then we see the astonishing phenomenon of Konstantin Leontiev—by nature a man of the sixteenth-century Renaissance who wandered into nineteenth-century Russia, into a world so alien and opposite to the Renaissance, living out a sad and suffering fate within it.

Finally, the summits of Russian literature—Tolstoy and Dostoevsky. There is nothing of the Renaissance in them. They are stricken with religious pain and torment; they seek salvation. This is characteristic of Russian creators; it is very national in them—they seek salvation, thirst for redemption, suffer over the world. In Dostoevsky, Russian literature reaches its summit, and in his creative work this anguished and religiously serious character of Russian literature is revealed. In Dostoevsky all the darkness of Russian life, of Russian fate, is concentrated, yet in this darkness a light has begun to shine.

The sorrowful path of Russian literature, filled to overflowing with religious pain and religious seeking, had to lead to Dostoevsky. But in Dostoevsky a breakthrough into other worlds already occurs; light is visible. Dostoevsky's tragedy, like all true tragedy, has catharsis—purification and liberation. Those who are cast by him exclusively into *gloom and* hopelessness, whom he torments without bringing joy, do not see and do not know Dostoevsky. There is great joy in reading Dostoevsky, great liberation of spirit. It is joy through suffering. But such is the Christian path.

Dostoevsky restores faith in man, in the depths of man. This faith does not exist in shallow humanism. Humanism destroys man. Man is reborn when he believes in God. Faith in man is faith in Christ, in the God-Man. Throughout his entire life Dostoevsky carried an exceptional, unique feeling for Christ, a kind of ecstatic love for the countenance of Christ. In the name of Christ, out of boundless love for Christ, Dostoevsky broke with that humanistic world of which Belinsky was the prophet.

Dostoevsky's faith in Christ passed through the crucible of all doubts and was tempered in fire. He writes in his notebook: "And in Europe there have never been atheistic expressions of such force. It follows, then, that I do not believe in Christ and profess Him like a boy. My Hosanna has passed through a great crucible of doubt." Dostoevsky lost his youthful faith in "Schiller"—by this name he symbolically designated all that is "lofty and beautiful," idealistic humanism. Faith in "Schiller" did not withstand the test; faith in Christ withstood all tests. He lost the humanistic faith in man, but remained faithful to the Christian faith in man—he deepened, strengthened, and enriched this faith.

And therefore Dostoevsky could not be a gloomy, hopelessly pessimistic writer. Liberating light is present even in Dostoevsky's darkest and most tormenting works. This is the light of Christ, which shines even in the darkness. Dostoevsky leads man through the abysses of division—division is the fundamental motif of Dostoevsky—but division does not ultimately destroy man. Through the God-Man the human image can be restored anew.

Dostoevsky belongs to those writers who succeeded in revealing themselves in their artistic creation. In his creative work all the contradictions of his spirit, all his bottomless depths, are reflected. For him, creativity was not, as it is for many, a concealment of what was occurring in the depths. He concealed nothing, and therefore he succeeded in making astonishing discoveries about man. In the fate of his heroes he tells of his own fate, in their doubts—of his own doubts, in their divisions—of his own divisions, in their criminal experience—of the secret crimes of his own spirit.

Dostoevsky's biography is less interesting than his creative work. Dostoevsky's letters are less interesting than his novels. He put his whole self into his works. And through them one can study him. Therefore Dostoevsky is less enigmatic than many other writers; he is easier to decipher than, for example, Gogol. Gogol is one of the most enigmatic of Russian writers. He did not reveal himself in his creative work; he carried the mystery of his personality with him into another world. And it is unlikely that anyone will ever fully decipher it. Such an enigma will the personality of Vladimir Solovyov remain for us. In his philosophical and theological treatises, in his journalism, Vladimir Solovyov concealed rather than revealed himself; the contradictory nature of his personality is not reflected in them. Only from individual poems can one guess at something. Dostoevsky is not like this. The peculiarity of his genius was such that he succeeded in telling to the depths, through his creative work, of his own fate—which is at the same time the cosmic fate of man. He did not hide from us his Sodom ideal, and he also revealed to us the heights of his Madonna ideal. Therefore Dostoevsky's creative work is a revelation. Dostoevsky's epilepsy is not a superficial illness; in it the very depths of his spirit are disclosed.

Dostoevsky liked to call himself a "man of the soil" and professed a soil-bound ideology. And this is true only in the sense that he was and remained a Russian man, organically connected with the Russian people. He never tore himself away from national roots. But he did not resemble the Slavophiles; he belonged to an entirely different epoch. Compared with the Slavophiles, Dostoevsky was a Russian wanderer, a Russian pilgrim through spiritual worlds. He had no home of his own and no land of his own, no cozy nest of landowners' estates. He was no longer bound to any statics of everyday life; he was entirely in dynamics, in restlessness, entirely permeated by currents flowing from the future, entirely in a revolution of the spirit. He was a man of the Apocalypse. The Slavophiles were not yet afflicted with the apocalyptic illness.

Dostoevsky above all depicted the fate of the Russian wanderer and outcast, and this is far more characteristic of him than his attachment to the soil. He considered this wandering to be a characteristic Russian trait. The Slavophiles, on the other hand, were squat people, rooted in the earth, people firmly attached to the land. And the very soil of the earth was still solid and firm beneath them. Dostoevsky is an underground man. His element is fire, not earth. His line is a whirlwind movement. And everything in Dostoevsky is already different from the Slavophiles. His attitude toward Western Europe is different—he is a patriot of Europe, not only of Russia; his attitude toward the Petrine period of Russian history is different—he is a writer of the Petersburg period, an artist of Petersburg. The Slavophiles were in an integral way of life. Dostoevsky is already entirely in division. We shall yet see how Dostoevsky's ideas about Russia differ from those of the Slavophiles. But I would like to establish at once that Dostoevsky is not of the Slavophile breed.

In his everyday appearance, Dostoevsky was a very typical Russian writer, a man of letters who lived by his labor. He cannot be conceived outside of literature. He lived by literature both spiritually and materially. He was connected with nothing except literature. And in his person he manifested the bitter fate of the Russian writer.

Truly astonishing is Dostoevsky's mind, extraordinary is the sharpness of his intellect. He is one of the most intelligent writers in world literature. His mind not only corresponds to the power of his artistic gift, but perhaps surpasses his artistic gift. In this he differs greatly from Leo Tolstoy, who strikes one by the clumsiness, straightforwardness, and almost flatness of his mind, which does not stand at the level of his brilliant artistic gift. Of course, it was not Tolstoy but Dostoevsky who was the great thinker. Dostoevsky's creative work is an astonishing revelation of mind—brilliant, sparkling, penetrating.

In the power and sharpness of his mind, among great writers only one can be compared to him—Shakespeare, the great mind of the Renaissance. Even the mind of Goethe, the greatest of the great, did not possess such sharpness, such dialectical depth, as the mind of

Dostoevsky. And this is all the more astonishing because Dostoevsky dwells in a Dionysian, orgiastic element. This element, when it entirely seizes hold of a person, usually does not favor the sharpness and keenness of the mind; it clouds the mind. But in Dostoevsky we see an orgiastic quality, an ecstatic quality in thought itself; his very dialectic of ideas is Dionysian.

Dostoevsky is intoxicated with thought; he is entirely in a fiery whirlwind of thought. The dialectic of ideas in Dostoevsky intoxicates, but in this intoxication the sharpness of thought does not fade—thought reaches its ultimate acuity. Those who are not interested in Dostoevsky's dialectic of ideas, in the tragic paths of his brilliant thought, for whom he is merely an artist and psychologist—they do not know much in Dostoevsky; they cannot understand his spirit.

All of Dostoevsky's creative work is the artistic resolution of an ideational task, a tragic movement of ideas. The Underground Man is an idea; Raskolnikov is an idea; Stavrogin, Kirillov, Shatov, Pyotr Verkhovensky are ideas; Ivan Karamazov is an idea. All of Dostoevsky's heroes are absorbed by some idea, intoxicated by an idea; all the conversations in his novels represent an astonishing dialectic of ideas. Everything written by Dostoevsky is written about the "accursed" questions of the world.

This in no way means that Dostoevsky wrote tendentious novels with a thesis to advance certain ideas. Ideas are entirely immanent to his artistry; he artistically reveals the life of ideas. He is an "ideational" writer in the Platonic sense of the word, and not in that disagreeable sense in which this expression was usually used in our criticism. He contemplates primal ideas, but always in movement, in dynamics, in their tragic fate, and not in repose.

Of himself Dostoevsky said very modestly: "I am weak in philosophy (but not in love for it—in love for it I am strong)." This means that academic philosophy came to him with difficulty. His intuitive genius knew its own paths of philosophizing. He was a true philosopher, the greatest Russian philosopher. For philosophy he gives infinitely much. Philosophical thought must be saturated with his contemplations. Dostoevsky's creative work is infinitely important for philosophical anthropology, for the philosophy of history, for the philosophy of religion, for moral philosophy. He perhaps learned little from philosophy, but he can teach it much, and we have long been philosophizing about ultimate things under the sign of Dostoevsky. Only philosophizing about penultimate things is bound up with traditional philosophy.

Dostoevsky opens up a new spiritual world; he restores to man his spiritual depth. This spiritual depth was taken from man and cast off into a transcendent distance, into heights unattainable for him. And man was left in the middle realm of his soul and on the surface of his body. He ceased to feel the dimension of depth. This process of alienating man's deep spiritual world from him begins in the religious-ecclesiastical sphere, as a distancing into an exclusively transcendent world of one's spiritual life and the creation of religion for the soul that strives toward this spiritual world taken from it. This process ends in positivism, agnosticism, and materialism—that is, in the complete despiritualizing of man and the world.

The transcendent world is finally banished into the unknowable. All paths of communication are cut off, and in the end this world is altogether denied.

The hostility of official Christianity toward all gnosticism had to end in the affirmation of agnosticism; the casting out of man's spiritual depth had to lead to the denial of all spiritual experience, to the enclosure of man within "material" and "psychological" reality. Dostoevsky as a phenomenon of spirit signifies a turn inward, toward the spiritual depth of man, toward spiritual experience—a return to man of his own spiritual depth, a breakthrough through the enclosed "material" and "psychological" reality. For him, man is not only a "psychological" but a spiritual being. Spirit is not outside man but inside man.

Dostoevsky affirms the boundlessness of spiritual experience; he removes all limitations, sweeps away all guard posts. Spiritual distances are disclosed in an inner, immanent movement. In man and through man, God is comprehended. Therefore Dostoevsky can be recognized as an immanentist in the deepest sense of the word. This is the path of freedom that Dostoevsky opens. He reveals Christ in the depths of man, through man's suffering path, through freedom. Dostoevsky's religion is, by its type, opposed to the authoritarian-transcendent type of religiosity. It is the freest religion the world has seen, breathing the pathos of freedom.

In his religious consciousness Dostoevsky never attained final wholeness, never overcame contradictions to the end; he was on the way. But his positive pathos lay in an unprecedented religion of freedom and free love. In *A Writer's Diary* one can find passages that will seem to contradict such an understanding of Dostoevsky. But it must be said that *A Writer's Diary* also contains all of Dostoevsky's basic ideas, scattered in various places. These ideas are then repeated with still greater force in his novels. There already exists there the ideational dialectic of "The Legend of the Grand Inquisitor," in which the religion of freedom is affirmed.

Contrary to a frequently expressed opinion, one must energetically insist that the direction of Dostoevsky's spirit was positive, not negative. His pathos was a pathos of affirmation, not negation. He accepted God, man, and the world through all the torments of division and darkness. Dostoevsky understood to the depths the nature of Russian nihilism. But if he denied anything, he denied nihilism. He is an anti-nihilist. And this distinguishes him from Leo Tolstoy, who was infected with nihilistic negation.

Today Dostoevsky has become closer to us than ever before. We have once again drawn near to him. And much that is new is revealed in him for us in light of our knowledge of the tragic Russian fate we have lived through.

Chapter II.
Man

Dostoevsky had only one all-consuming interest, only one theme to which he devoted all his creative powers. This theme is man and his destiny. One cannot help but be struck by Dostoevsky's exceptional anthropologism and anthropocentrism. There is something frenzied and exclusive in Dostoevsky's absorption with man. For him, man is not a phenomenon of the natural world, not one phenomenon among others in a series, even if the highest. Man is a microcosm, the center of being, the sun around which everything revolves. Everything is in man and for man. In man lies the riddle of world-life. To resolve the question of man means to resolve the question of God as well. All of Dostoevsky's creative work is an advocacy for man and his destiny, carried to the point of rebellion against God, yet resolving itself in the entrusting of man's destiny to the God-man—Christ.

Such an exclusive anthropological consciousness is possible only in the Christian world, only in the Christian epoch of history. The ancient world knew no such relation to man. It was Christianity that turned the whole world toward man and made man the sun of the world. And Dostoevsky's anthropologism is a profoundly Christian anthropologism. It is precisely Dostoevsky's exceptional relation to man that makes him a Christian writer. Humanists do not know such a relation to man; for them, man is merely a natural being. And we shall see that Dostoevsky exposes the inner defectiveness of humanism, its powerlessness to resolve the tragedy of human destiny.

In Dostoevsky there is nothing besides man: no nature, no world of things, and within man himself nothing that connects him with the natural world, with the world of things, with everyday life, with the objective order of existence. Only the human spirit exists, and only it is of interest; only it is investigated. N. Strakhov, who knew Dostoevsky closely, says of him: "All his attention was directed toward people, and he grasped only their nature and character. He was interested in people, exclusively people, with the constitution of their souls and the manner of their lives, their feelings and thoughts." During Dostoevsky's trip abroad, "Dostoevsky was not especially occupied with either nature, or historical monuments, or works of art."

True, in Dostoevsky there is the city, there are urban slums, dirty taverns and fetid furnished rooms. But the city is merely the atmosphere of man, merely a moment in the tragic destiny of man; the city is permeated by man but has no independent existence—it is only man's backdrop. Man has fallen away from nature, torn himself from organic roots, and ended up in repulsive urban slums, where he writhes in torment. The city is the tragic destiny of man. The city of Petersburg, which Dostoevsky felt and described so astonishingly, is a phantom engendered by man in his apostasy and wandering. In the atmosphere of fogs of this phantasmal city, mad thoughts are born; designs of crimes ripen in which the boundaries of human nature are transgressed. Everything is concentrated and condensed around man, who has torn himself away from the divine first-foundations. Everything external—the city and its peculiar atmosphere, rooms and their ugly furnishings, taverns with their stench and filth, the external plots of the novels—all this is merely signs, symbols of the inner, spiritual human world, merely reflections of inner human destiny. Nothing external—natural or social, everyday—has for Dostoevsky any independent reality.

The dirty taverns in which "Russian boys" carry on conversations about world questions are merely symbolically reflected moments of the human spirit and of the dialectic of ideas organically fused with that destiny. And all the complexity of plots, all the everyday multiplicity of characters colliding in passionate attraction or repulsion, in a whirlwind of passions, is merely a reflection of the destiny of the single human spirit in its inner depths. All of this revolves around the riddle of man; all of it is needed to reveal the inner moments of his destiny.

In the construction of Dostoevsky's novels there is a very pronounced centralization. Everyone and everything is directed toward one central person, or this central person is directed toward everyone and everything. This person is a riddle, and everyone tries to solve his secret. Everyone is drawn by this enigmatic mystery. Take *The Adolescent*, one of Dostoevsky's most remarkable and insufficiently appreciated creations. Everything revolves around the central figure of Versilov, one of the most captivating images in Dostoevsky; everything is saturated with a passionate relation to him—attraction to or repulsion from him. Everyone has only one "business"—to solve the secret of Versilov, the riddle of his personality, his strange destiny. The contradictoriness of Versilov's nature strikes everyone. And no one can find peace until he has solved the secret of Versilov's nature. This is the real, serious, profoundly human "business" with which everyone is occupied.

In Dostoevsky, people are never occupied with other "business." From an ordinary point of view, Dostoevsky's heroes might give the impression of idlers. But the relationship between people is the most serious, the only serious "business." Man is higher than any "business." Man is the only "business." No other "business," no life-building can be found in the infinitely diverse human kingdom of Dostoevsky. A kind of center forms, a central human personality, and everything revolves around this axis. A whirlwind of passionate human relationships forms, and everyone is drawn into it. Everyone spins frenziedly in this whirlwind. This whirlwind rises from the very depths of human nature—from the underground, volcanic nature of man, from human bottomlessness.

What is the adolescent, Versilov's illegitimate son, occupied with? What does he fuss about from morning to evening; where is he always hurrying without respite or rest? For whole days he runs from one person to another to learn Versilov's "secret," to solve the riddle of his personality. And this is serious "business." Everyone feels Versilov's significance, and everyone is struck by the contradictions of his nature. Everyone notices the deep irrationality in his character. A life-riddle about Versilov has been posed. This is a riddle about man, about human destiny. Because in the complex, contradictory, irrational character of Versilov, in the destiny of this extraordinary man, is hidden the riddle about man in general. And it seems that there is nothing besides Versilov; everything exists only for him and in relation to him; everything merely signifies his inner destiny.

The same centralized construction is characteristic of *Demons*. Stavrogin is the sun around which everything revolves. And around Stavrogin a whirlwind rises that passes into demonic frenzy. Everyone is drawn to him as to the sun; everything proceeds from him and returns to him; everything is merely his destiny. Shatov, P. Verkhovensky, Kirillov are merely parts of Stavrogin's disintegrated personality, merely emanations of this extraordinary personality in which it exhausts itself. The riddle of Stavrogin, the secret of Stavrogin, is the sole theme of *Demons*. The only "business" with which everyone is absorbed is the "case" of Stavrogin. The revolutionary demonic frenzy is merely a moment of Stavrogin's destiny, a signification of Stavrogin's inner reality, his self-will.

The depth of man in Dostoevsky can never be expressed and revealed in stable everyday life; it is always disclosed in a fiery torrent in which all stable forms melt and burn up, all cooled and frozen everyday structures. Thus Dostoevsky introduces us into the very depths of the contradictions of human nature, contradictions covered by the external veil of everyday life in artists of a different type. The disclosure of human depth leads to catastrophe, beyond the limits of the well-ordered arrangements of this world. Thus in *Demons* is revealed the disintegration of an extraordinary human personality that has exhausted its powers in the boundlessness of its strivings, incapable of choice and sacrifice.

The conception of *The Idiot* is opposite to the conception of *The Adolescent* and *Demons*. In *The Idiot*, all movement goes not toward the central figure of Prince Myshkin but from him toward everyone. Myshkin solves the riddle of everyone, above all of the two women—Nastasya Filippovna and Aglaya—and is full of prophetic presentiments, intuitive insights. He goes to help everyone. Human relationships are the only "business" by which he is wholly seized. He himself lives in quiet ecstasy. Around him are stormy whirlwinds.

The enigmatically irrational, "demonic" principle in Stavrogin and Versilov intensifies and heats the surrounding atmosphere, engenders around itself a demonic spinning. The equally irrational but "angelic" principle in Myshkin does not engender demonic frenzy from itself, but it cannot cure people of demonic frenzy, though Myshkin with all his soul wants to be a healer. Myshkin is not fully, not entirely a man; his nature is luminous but deficient. Later, Dostoevsky will attempt to show the complete man in Alyosha.

It is very interesting that while the "dark" ones—Stavrogin, Versilov, Ivan Karamazov—are solved as riddles, and everyone moves toward them, the "luminous" ones—Myshkin, Alyosha—themselves solve the riddles of others; movement goes from them toward everyone. Alyosha solves Ivan ("Ivan is a riddle"); Myshkin sees into the soul of Nastasya Filippovna and Aglaya. The "luminous" ones—Myshkin, Alyosha—are endowed with the gift of insight; they go to help people. The "dark" ones—Stavrogin, Versilov, Ivan Karamazov—

are endowed with an enigmatic nature that torments and agonizes everyone. Such is the conception of centripetal and centrifugal movement in Dostoevsky's novels.

The conception of *Crime and Punishment* is different. There, human destiny is revealed not in human multiplicity, not in the incandescent atmosphere of human interrelations. Raskolnikov solves the riddle of the boundaries of human nature alone with himself; he experiments upon his own nature. The "dark" Raskolnikov was not yet a "riddle" like Stavrogin or Ivan. This is still a stage in the destiny of man, in the paths of human self-will, preceding Stavrogin and Ivan Karamazov—less complex. It is not Raskolnikov himself who is enigmatic; it is his crime that is enigmatic. Man transgresses his own boundaries. But self-will has not yet fundamentally altered human nature. The hero of *Notes from Underground* and Raskolnikov pose problems and riddles. Versilov, Ivan Karamazov, Stavrogin are themselves problems and riddles.

Dostoevsky is above all a great anthropologist, an experimenter upon human nature. He opens up a new science of man and applies to it a new method, unprecedented until now. The artistic science or scientific artistry of Dostoevsky investigates human nature in its bottomlessness and boundlessness, uncovers its ultimate, subterranean layers. Dostoevsky subjects man to spiritual experiment, places him in exceptional conditions, tears away all external accretions, tearing man away from all everyday foundations. He conducts his anthropological investigations through the method of Dionysian artistry, drawing one into the mysterious depth of human nature; into this depth one is drawn by an ecstatic, frenzied whirlwind.

All of Dostoevsky's creative work is a whirlwind anthropology. In it, everything is disclosed in an ecstatically fiery atmosphere; access to Dostoevsky's knowledge is granted only to those who are drawn into this whirlwind. In Dostoevsky's anthropology there is nothing static, nothing frozen, nothing petrified; everything in it is dynamic, everything in movement, everything a torrent of incandescent lava. Dostoevsky lures one into the dark abyss that opens within man himself. He leads through utter darkness. But even in this darkness, light must shine forth. He wants to extract light from darkness.

Dostoevsky takes man released into freedom, emerged from under the law, fallen out of the cosmic order, and investigates his destiny in freedom, reveals the inescapable results of the paths of freedom. Dostoevsky is above all interested in the destiny of man in freedom that passes into self-will. Here is where human nature is revealed. Man's existence under the law, on firm earthly soil, does not disclose the secrets of human nature. Dostoevsky becomes especially interested in the destiny of man at the moment when he has rebelled against the objective world-order, torn himself from nature, from organic roots, and declared his self-will. The apostate from natural, organic life is cast by Dostoevsky into the purgatory and hell of the city, and there he passes through his path of suffering, expiating his guilt.

It is very instructive to compare the relation to man in Dante, Shakespeare, and Dostoevsky. In Dante, man is an organic part of an objective world-order, a divine cosmos. He is a member of a hierarchical system. Above him is heaven; below him is hell. God and the devil are realities of the world-order given to man from outside. The circles of hell with their terrible torments only confirm the existence of such an objective divine world-order. God and the devil, heaven and hell are revealed not in the depths of the human spirit, not in the bottomlessness of spiritual experience, but are given to man, possessing a reality similar to the realities of the objective material world. Such is the medieval worldview, still closely connected with the worldview of ancient man. Man sensed above himself a heaven with a heavenly hierarchy, and beneath himself the netherworld. Dante was the brilliant expresser of the world-perception of medieval man. The cosmos as a hierarchical organism was not yet shaken; man firmly abided within it.

From the epoch of the Renaissance, from the beginning of the modern age, the contemplation of the world radically changes. Humanistic self-affirmation of man begins. Man encloses himself in his natural world. Heaven and the netherworld close for the new man. The infinity of worlds opens up, but there is no longer a single, hierarchically organized cosmos. The infinite and empty astronomical sky no longer resembles the sky of Dante, the sky of the Middle Ages. And understandable is the horror that the infinity of spaces inspired in Pascal. Man is lost in these infinite spaces that have no cosmic structure. But he withdraws into his own vast human psychic world; he clings still more firmly to the earth, fears to tear himself away from it, fears the infinity alien to him.

The humanistic epoch of modern history begins, in which the creative powers of man are lived out. Man felt himself free, not chained to any objective cosmic order given from outside. Shakespeare was one of the greatest geniuses of the Renaissance. His creative work reveals for the first time the infinitely complex and multifarious human psychic world, the world of human passions, the effervescent play of human powers, full of energy and might. Dante's heaven, Dante's hell no longer exist in Shakespeare's creative work. Man's position in Shakespeare is determined by the humanistic worldview. This humanistic worldview is turned toward the psychic world of man, not toward the spiritual world, not toward the ultimate spiritual depth. Man moves to the periphery of psychic life, tears himself away from spiritual centers. Shakespeare was the greatest psychologist of humanistic art.

Dostoevsky appears in a different world-epoch, in a different age of man. In him too, man no longer belongs to that objective cosmic order to which Dante's man belonged. Man in modern history attempted to settle himself definitively on the surface of the earth; he enclosed himself in his purely human world. God and the devil, heaven and hell were definitively pushed into the sphere of the unknowable, with which there are no paths of communication, and finally were deprived of all reality. Man became a two-dimensional, flat being; he was deprived of the dimension of depth. He was left with only soul, but spirit departed from him. The creative powers of the Renaissance epoch proved to be exhausted. The joy of the Renaissance disappeared, the play of superabundant creative powers. And man felt that the ground beneath him was not as firm and unshakable as it had seemed to him.

From the closed dimension of depth, underground rumblings began to be heard; the volcanic nature of the subsoil began to be revealed. An abyss opened in the depths of man himself, and there God and the devil, heaven and hell were discovered anew. But the first movements into the depth had to be movements in darkness; the daylight of the psychic human world and of the material world toward which it was turned began to fade, while a new light had not yet been kindled. All of modern history was a trial of human freedom; in it, human powers were released into freedom. But at the end of this historical epoch, the trial of human freedom is transferred to a greater depth, into another dimension, and there human destiny is tested. The paths of human freedom from the psychic world, illuminated by the daylight of modern history, are transferred into the spiritual world. And this spiritual world had at first to produce the impression of a descent into the netherworld. There God and heaven will once again be disclosed to man, and not only the devil and hell—but not as an objective order given to man from outside, rather as an encounter with the ultimate depth of the human spirit, as realities opening from within. This is precisely Dostoevsky's creative work.

In him, man occupies an essentially different position than in Dante and Shakespeare. He does not belong to an objective order, but he does not remain on the surface of the earth and on the surface of his soul. Spiritual life returns to man, but from the depths, from within, through darkness, through purgatory and hell. Therefore Dostoevsky's path is a path of spiritual immanence, not transcendence. This does not mean, of course, that he denied the reality of the transcendent.

Man's path in freedom begins with extreme individualism, with isolation, with rebellion against the external world-order. Boundless self-love develops; the underground is revealed. Man passes from the surface of the earth into the underground. The underground man appears—an unseemly, ugly man—and unfolds his dialectic. Here for the first time, in the brilliant dialectic of ideas of *Notes from Underground*, Dostoevsky makes a whole series of discoveries about human nature.

Human nature is polar, antinomian, and irrational. Man has an ineradicable need for the irrational, for mad freedom, for suffering. Man does not necessarily strive for profit. In his self-will, man more often than not prefers suffering. He does not reconcile himself to a rational ordering of life. Freedom is higher than well-being. But freedom is not the dominion of reason over the elemental forces of the soul; freedom is itself irrational and mad; it draws one toward transgressing the limits set for man. This boundless freedom torments man, draws him toward destruction. But man treasures this torment and this destruction.

The discoveries about man made by Dostoevsky in the "underground" determine the destiny of Raskolnikov, Stavrogin, Ivan Karamazov, and others. The suffering wandering of man on the paths of self-willed freedom begins. And it brings man to the ultimate limits of division. The ideational dialectic about man and his destiny begins in *Notes from Underground*, will be further revealed through all of Dostoevsky's novels, and will find its completion in the "Legend of the Grand Inquisitor." Ivan Karamazov will be the final stage of the path of freedom that has passed into self-will and rebellion against God. After this will appear the images of Zosima and Alyosha. We shall see that the whole tragic dialectic about man is resolved by the image of Christ in the Legend. With what, then, does it begin?

The underground man rejects any rational organization of universal harmony and well-being. "I should not be in the least surprised," says the hero of *Notes from Underground*, "if suddenly, for no apparent reason, in the midst of the universal future good sense some gentleman with an ignoble or, better said, retrograde and mocking physiognomy were to arise, set his arms akimbo, and say to us all: 'Well, gentlemen, what if we were to kick all this good sense over with one blow, into the dust, for the sole purpose of sending all these logarithms to the devil and living again according to our own stupid will' (emphasis mine—N.B.). This would still be nothing, but what is offensive is that he would certainly find followers; that is how man is constituted.

"And all this from the most trifling cause, which would seem not worth mentioning: namely, that man, always and everywhere, whoever he may be, has preferred to act as he chose, and not at all as reason and advantage dictated; and one may choose what is contrary to one's own advantage, and sometimes one positively ought to. One's own free and unfettered willing, one's own caprice however wild, one's fancy irritated sometimes to the point of madness—this is precisely that most advantageous advantage, overlooked and defying classification, which constantly sends all systems and theories to the devil.

"And where did all these sages get the idea that man needs some kind of normal, some kind of virtuous willing? Why have they positively imagined that man necessarily needs reasonably advantageous willing? Man needs only one thing—*independent* willing, whatever that independence may cost and wherever it may lead." "There is only one case, only one, when man may deliberately, consciously desire for himself even what is harmful, stupid, even the stupidest thing—namely, in order to have the right to desire for himself even the stupidest thing and not to be bound by the obligation to desire only what is sensible. After all, this stupidest thing, this caprice of ours, may in fact, gentlemen, be more advantageous to our kind than anything else on earth, particularly in certain cases. And in particular it may be more advantageous than all other advantages, even when it brings us obvious harm and contradicts the soundest conclusions of our reason concerning advantage—because in any case *it preserves for us the most important and most precious thing, that is, our personality and our individuality*" (emphasis mine—N.B.).

Man is not arithmetic; man is a problematic and enigmatic being. The nature of man is antinomian and polar to its very depths. "What can be expected of man as a being endowed with such strange qualities? Man will desire the most pernicious nonsense, the most uneconomical absurdity, solely in order to add to all this positive good sense his own pernicious fantastic element. It is precisely his fantastic dreams, his most vulgar stupidity that he will want to retain for himself solely in order to confirm to himself that people are still people and not piano keys." "If you say that even this can be calculated by a table, both the chaos and the darkness and the curses, so that the very possibility of preliminary calculation would stop everything and reason would prevail—well, man would deliberately go mad in that case, in order to be without reason and to insist on his own. I believe in this, I answer for this, because after all the whole human affair, it seems, really does consist only in this—that *man should constantly prove to himself that he is a man and not an organ-stop*" (emphasis mine—N.B.).

"What kind of free will is left when it comes to tables and arithmetic, when there will be nothing but twice two makes four? Twice two makes four without my will. Is that really what free will is?" "Perhaps man loves destruction and chaos so much precisely because he instinctively fears attaining his goal and completing the building under construction? And who knows—perhaps the entire goal on earth to which humanity strives consists only in this continual process of attainment, in other words, in *life itself*, and not properly in the goal, which of course must be nothing other than twice two makes four—that is, a formula—and after all, *twice two makes four is no longer life, gentlemen, but the beginning of death*" (emphasis mine—N.B.).

"And why are you so firmly, so triumphantly convinced that only the normal and positive—in a word, only well-being—is advantageous to man? Does not reason err concerning advantages? After all, perhaps man loves not only well-being; perhaps he loves suffering just as much, to the point of passion... I am convinced that man will never renounce genuine suffering, that is, destruction and chaos. Suffering—why, this is the sole cause of consciousness."

In these thoughts, staggering in their genius, in their acuity of mind, one must seek the primary source of all the discoveries that Dostoevsky makes about man throughout his entire creative path. To man must be applied not arithmetic but higher mathematics. Human destiny is never based on the truth that twice two makes four. Human nature can never be rationalized. An irrational remainder always remains, and in it lies the source of life.

Nor is it possible to rationalize human society. In society too, the irrational principle always remains and acts. Human society is not an anthill, and human freedom—which is drawn toward "living according to one's own stupid will"—will not permit the transformation of society into an anthill. The gentleman with the retrograde and mocking physiognomy is the revolt of personality, of the individual principle, the revolt of freedom that permits no coercive rationalization, no imposed well-being.

Here is already determined Dostoevsky's deep hostility to socialism, to the Crystal Palace, to the utopia of earthly paradise. This will later be revealed in its depths in *Demons* and in *The Brothers Karamazov*. Man cannot allow himself to be turned into a "piano key" and an "organ-stop." Dostoevsky had a frenzied feeling for personality. His entire worldview is permeated by personalism. Connected with this was the problem of immortality, central for him. Dostoevsky is a brilliant critic of modern eudaemonism; he reveals its incompatibility with the freedom and dignity of personality.

Was Dostoevsky himself an underground man? Did he ideologically sympathize with the dialectic of the underground man? This question cannot be posed or resolved statically; it must be resolved dynamically. The worldview of the underground man is not Dostoevsky's positive worldview. In his positive religious worldview, Dostoevsky exposes the ruinous nature of the paths of self-will and rebellion taken by the underground man. Such self-will and rebellion lead to the destruction of human freedom and the disintegration of personality. Yet the underground man, with his astonishing ideological dialectic concerning irrational human freedom, represents a moment in the tragic path of humanity—the path of living through freedom and testing freedom. Freedom is the highest good; a person cannot renounce it without ceasing to be human.

What the underground man negates in his dialectic, Dostoevsky himself also negates in his positive worldview. He will reject to the end the rationalization of human society; he will reject to the end every attempt to place well-being, prudence, and prosperity above freedom; he will reject the coming Crystal Palace, the coming harmony founded upon the annihilation of human personality. But he will lead humanity further along the paths of self-will and rebellion in order to reveal that in self-will freedom is destroyed, and in rebellion the human being is negated.

The path of freedom leads either to man-godhood, on which path a person finds their end and their ruin, or to God-manhood, on which path a person finds salvation and the ultimate affirmation of their image. A human being exists only if they are the image and likeness of God, only if God exists. If there is no God, if a person is themselves a god, then there is no human being either—their image perishes as well. Only in Christ is the problem of humanity resolved.

The ideological dialectic of the underground man is merely the initial moment of Dostoevsky's own ideological dialectic; it begins there but does not end there. It reaches its positive completion in *The Brothers Karamazov*. But one thing remains beyond doubt: there is no return to that enslaved, coercively rationalized consciousness against which the underground man rebels. Humanity must pass through freedom. And Dostoevsky shows how, when a person is forcibly crammed into rationalistic frameworks and their life is distributed according to tables, they will "deliberately go mad just for this occasion, so as to have no reason and to insist on their own way." He recognizes the "fantastic element" in the human being as essential to human nature. Stavrogin, Versilov, and Ivan Karamazov will remain "enigmas" because human nature in general is enigmatic in its antinomian character, in its irrationality, in its need for suffering.

In his anthropology, Dostoevsky discovers that human nature is dynamic in the highest degree; in its depths lies fiery movement. Repose and stasis exist only in the uppermost, most superficial layer of the human being. Behind settled everyday life, behind the soul's seemly composure, storms are concealed and dark abysses yawn open. Dostoevsky is interested in human beings when they have already entered a state of turbulent movement. He descends into these dark abysses and there extracts light. Light is not only for the seemly surface; light can also shine in the dark abyss, and this is a more authentic light.

This fiery movement within the human being arises from the polarity of human nature, from the collision of opposites hidden within it. Polarity and antinomy extend to the very depth of human nature. In the deepest depth there is not repose, not unity, but passionate movement. Dostoevsky does not contemplate the repose of eternity in the depths. In this, Dostoevsky's contemplation differs greatly from Plato's, from the contemplation of many mystics. The turbulent collision of polar opposites occurs not only on the bodily and psychic plane but on the spiritual plane as well. Movement seizes not only the surface of being but being's very depth. This is essential to Dostoevsky's anthropology and ontology. In this he is the opposite of the aesthetic worldview of Hellenic genius. He belongs to the Christian world, in which the tragic dynamic of being has been definitively revealed.

The Russian, Slavic genius does not coincide in its contemplation of being's ultimate depths with the Germanic genius as reflected in German idealism. The German is inclined to see the collision of God and the devil, of light and darkness, on the periphery of being; but when he goes into the depth of spiritual life, he sees God there, contemplates light—polarity disappears. In the Russian Dostoevsky, the polarity of the divine and the diabolical principle, the turbulent collision of light and darkness, is revealed in the very depth of being. God and the devil struggle in the deepest depths of the human spirit. Evil has a deep, spiritual nature. The battlefield of God and the devil is laid very deep within human nature.

Dostoevsky perceived tragic contradiction not in that psychic sphere where everyone sees it, but in the abyss of being itself. The tragedy of polarity extends, as it were, into the very depth of divine life. And the distinction between the "divine" and the "diabolical" in Dostoevsky does not coincide with the ordinary, peripheral distinction between "good" and "evil." If Dostoevsky had fully disclosed his teaching about God, about the Absolute, he would have been compelled to acknowledge polarity in the divine nature itself, a dark nature, an abyss in God—something akin to Jakob Böhme's teaching about the Ungrund. The human heart is polar in its very foundation, but the human heart is lodged in the bottomless depth of being.

To Dostoevsky belongs the astonishing statement that "beauty will save the world." For him there was nothing higher than beauty. Beauty is divine—yet even beauty, that supreme image of ontological perfection, appears to Dostoevsky as polar, doubled, contradictory, terrible, and frightening. He does not contemplate the divine repose of beauty, its Platonic idea; he sees in it fiery movement, tragic collision. Beauty was revealed to him through the human being. He does not contemplate beauty in the cosmos, in the divine world-order. Hence there is eternal disquiet even in beauty itself. There is no repose in humanity. Beauty is caught up in the Heraclitean current.

Too well known are these words of Mitya Karamazov: "Beauty is a terrible and frightening thing. Terrible because it is indefinable, and it cannot be defined because God has set only riddles. Here the shores converge, here all contradictions live together... Beauty. Moreover, I cannot bear it that a man of lofty heart and high mind begins with the ideal of the Madonna and ends with the ideal of Sodom. What is still more terrible is when one who already has the ideal of Sodom in their soul does not deny the ideal of the Madonna, and their heart burns from it—truly, truly burns, as in innocent, youthful years. No, humanity is broad, too broad even; I would narrow it." And further: "Beauty is not only a terrible but also a mysterious thing. Here the devil struggles with God, and the battlefield is the hearts of people."

And Nikolai Stavrogin "found in both poles a coincidence of beauty, an identical pleasure"; he felt equal attraction to the ideal of the Madonna and the ideal of Sodom. Dostoevsky was tormented by the fact that beauty exists not only in the ideal of the Madonna but also in the ideal of Sodom. He sensed that even in beauty there is a dark, demonic principle. We shall see that he found a dark, evil principle even in love for people. So deep did his contemplation of the polarity of human nature extend.

Is this splitting and polarization of human nature, this tragic movement reaching into the very spiritual depth, into the most ultimate layers, not connected in Dostoevsky with the fact that he was called, at the end of modern history, on the threshold of some new world epoch, to reveal in humanity a struggle between God-man and man-god principles, between the principles of Christ and Antichrist—a struggle unknown to earlier epochs, in which evil appeared in a more elementary and simple form?

The soul of the person of our epoch has been loosened; everything has become unstable, everything appears doubled; one lives amid seductions and temptations, in perpetual danger of substitution. Evil appears in the guise of good and seduces. The image of Christ and of Antichrist, of God-man and man-god, is doubled. This is especially reflected in the work of Merezhkovsky, who simply cannot decide where Christ is and where Antichrist is. His book *L. Tolstoy and Dostoevsky*, remarkable in many respects, is permeated by this doubling, this constant substitution.

In our time many people have appeared with "divided thoughts," in whom the inner criteria of discernment have weakened. This is a human type discovered by Dostoevsky. Nothing can be done for this type with the old moral catechism; these souls require a more complex approach. Dostoevsky investigates the fate of these human souls permeated by the currents of an apocalyptic atmosphere. And this investigation opens up an enormous light. Dostoevsky takes the human being at a moment of deep spiritual crisis, of religious turning point. At this moment in a person's fate, a very essential discovery about human nature can be made. The phenomenon of Dostoevsky is an entirely new moment in anthropological consciousness. This consciousness is no longer merely traditionally Christian, neither patristic nor humanistic.

What, then, did Dostoevsky reveal that was new about the human being? He does not simply return to the old and eternal Christian truth about humanity after the humanistic falling away from it and forgetting of it. The experience of the humanistic period of history, the trial of human freedom, did not pass in vain. This was not pure loss and pure damage in human destiny. A new soul was born after this experience—with new doubts, with knowledge of new evil, but also with new horizons and distances, with a thirst for new communion with God. Humanity had already entered a different, more mature spiritual age.

And Dostoevsky's Christian—deeply Christian—anthropology differs already from patristic anthropology. The teaching about humanity held by the fathers and teachers of the Church, the teaching about the human path that is taught us by the life and writings of the saints, does not answer all the questions of the human being in their present spiritual age; it does not know all human doubts and temptations. Humanity has not become better, has not drawn closer to God, but its soul has become infinitely more complex and its consciousness more acute.

The old Christian soul knew sin and fell under the power of the devil. But it did not know that splitting of human personality which the soul investigated by Dostoevsky came to know. The old evil was clearer and simpler. The seductive and alluring paths of man-godhood had not yet opened before it as they opened before the souls of Raskolnikov, Stavrogin, Kirillov, and Ivan Karamazov. And it would be difficult to cure the modern soul of its spiritual ailments with the old remedies alone.

Dostoevsky knew this. He knew no less than Nietzsche knew, but he also knew what Nietzsche did not know. Dostoevsky's contemporary Theophan the Recluse, one of our most authoritative Orthodox-ascetic writers, did not know what Dostoevsky and Nietzsche knew, and therefore could not have answered the torment born of the new human experience. They came to know that humanity is terrifyingly free, and that this freedom is tragic, imposing a burden and suffering. And they saw the bifurcation of paths upward from the human being toward God-man and man-god.

The human soul stood revealed at the moment of its God-forsakenness, and this experience turned out to be a distinctive religious experience in which, after immersion in darkness, a new light is kindled. And therefore Dostoevsky's Christianity is very different from the Christianity of Theophan the Recluse. And therefore the elders of the Optina Hermitage did not fully recognize him as one of their own after reading *The Brothers Karamazov*. A path to Christ was opened through boundless freedom. The seductive lie of man-godhood is exposed on the very path of boundless freedom. And this was already a new word about the human being.

Dostoevsky's creative work signifies not only a crisis but the collapse of humanism, its inner exposure. In this, Dostoevsky's name must be placed alongside Nietzsche's. After Dostoevsky and Nietzsche, a return to the old rationalistic humanism is no longer possible; humanism has been surpassed. The humanistic self-assertion and self-satisfaction of the human being finds its end in Dostoevsky and Nietzsche. Beyond lies the path either to God-man or to superman, to man-god. One can no longer stop at the merely human.

Kirillov wants to become a god himself. Nietzsche wants to overcome humanity as a shame and disgrace and goes toward the superman. The ultimate limits of humanistic self-will and self-assertion lead to the destruction of the human being in the superman. In the superman the human being is not preserved; the human is overcome as a shame and disgrace, as weakness and nothingness. The human being is only a means for the appearance of the superman. The superman is an idol before whom the human being prostrates themselves, which devours the human being and all that is human. For one who has known the seduction of the superman, humanism can no longer be seductive. Humanism is the kingdom of the middle. European humanism spiritually ended in Nietzsche, who was flesh of its flesh and blood of its blood, and a sacrifice for its sins.

But before Nietzsche, in his brilliant dialectic about the human being, Dostoevsky revealed this fatal and inescapable end of humanism, this destruction of the human being on the path of man-godhood. There is an enormous difference between Dostoevsky and Nietzsche. Dostoevsky knew the seduction of man-godhood; he deeply investigated the paths of human self-will. But he knew something else: he saw the light of Christ, in which the darkness of man-godhood was exposed. He was spiritually sighted. Nietzsche, however, was himself in the grip of man-godhood ideas; the idea of the superman destroyed the human being in him. In Dostoevsky, the human being is preserved to the end.

In the man-god the human being perishes, and in the God-man the human being is preserved. Only Christianity saves the idea of the human being, forever preserving the human image. The being of humanity presupposes the being of God. The murder of God is the murder of humanity. On the grave of two great ideas—God and humanity (Christianity is the religion of God-man and God-manhood)—there rises up the image of a monster that kills God and humanity, the image of the coming man-god, the superman, the Antichrist. In Nietzsche there is neither God nor the human being, only an unknown superman. In Dostoevsky there is both God and the human being. God never absorbs the human being in him; the human being does not disappear in God but remains to the end and unto ages of ages. In this, Dostoevsky was a Christian in the deepest sense of the word.

It is astonishing that Dionysian ecstasy in Dostoevsky never leads to the disappearance of the human image, to the destruction of human individuality. In Greece, pagan Dionysianism led to the tearing apart of human individuality, to the disappearance of the human image in the faceless elemental force of nature. Dionysian ecstasies have always been dangerous for the human image. But no ecstasy, no frenzy in Dostoevsky leads to the negation of the human being. This is a very original trait in Dostoevsky.

Dostoevsky's anthropologism is an utterly exceptional and unprecedented phenomenon. The human image, the boundaries of personality, are not without reason associated with the Apollonian principle, with the principle of form. The Dionysian principle is usually understood as the abolition of the principle of individuation, the rupture of personal boundaries. In Dostoevsky it is otherwise. He is entirely Dionysian rather than Apollonian, existing in ecstasy and frenzy. Yet in this frenzied, ecstatic element, the human image, the human countenance, is affirmed with even greater force. The human being in their fiery polarity and dynamism remains in him down to the very depth; the human being is indestructible.

In this, Dostoevsky differs not only from Greek Dionysianism but also from many mystics of the Christian era, in whom only the divine remains and the human disappears. Dostoevsky wants to go to the very depth of divine life together with the human being. The human being belongs to the depth of eternity. And all of Dostoevsky's creative work is an intercession for the human being.

Dostoevsky's entire religious worldview is opposed to the spirit of Monophysitism. He recognizes to the end not one nature, divine or human, but two natures: both divine and human. And compared with Dostoevsky's religious anthropological consciousness, even Orthodox and Catholic consciousness may appear as an inclination toward Monophysitism, an absorption of human nature by divine nature. No one, it seems, in the history of the world has had such a relation to the human being as Dostoevsky.

Even in the lowest person, even in the most terrible human fall, the image and likeness of God is preserved. His love for the human being was not humanistic love. In this love he united boundless compassion with a certain cruelty. He preached to humanity a path of suffering. And this was connected with the fact that at the center of his anthropological consciousness lies the idea of freedom. Without freedom there is no human being. And Dostoevsky conducts his entire dialectic about humanity and its destiny as a dialectic about the destiny of freedom. But the path of freedom is a path of suffering. And this path of suffering must be traversed to the end by the human being. To fully know all that Dostoevsky revealed about humanity, one must turn to his investigation of freedom and evil.

Chapter III.
Freedom

For Dostoevsky, the theme of man and his destiny is first and foremost the theme of freedom. The fate of man, his suffering wanderings, are determined by his freedom. Freedom stands at the very center of Dostoevsky's worldview. And his deepest pathos is the pathos of freedom. It is astonishing that until now this has not been sufficiently recognized about Dostoevsky. Many passages from *The Diary of a Writer* are cited in which he supposedly opposed socio-political freedom, was a conservative and even a reactionary, and these entirely external approaches prevent people from seeing freedom as the very heart of all Dostoevsky's creative work, as the key to understanding his worldview.

What has been called Dostoevsky's "cruelty" is connected with his attitude toward freedom. He was "cruel" because he did not wish to lift from man the burden of freedom, did not wish to spare man suffering at the price of depriving him of freedom, and placed upon man an enormous responsibility corresponding to the dignity of the free. One could alleviate human torments by taking freedom away from man. And Dostoevsky investigates to the depths these paths, these paths of alleviating and ordering man without freedom of spirit.

Dostoevsky has truly brilliant thoughts about freedom, and they must be brought to light. For him, freedom is both anthropodicy and theodicy; in it one must seek both the justification of man and the justification of God. The entire world process is the posing of the theme of freedom; it is a tragedy bound up with the working out of this theme. Dostoevsky investigates the fate of man set free. He is interested only in the man who has taken the path of freedom, in the fate of man in freedom and of freedom in man. All his novels are tragedies—trials of human freedom. Man begins by defiantly asserting his freedom, ready for any suffering, for madness, if only to feel himself free. And at the same time man seeks ultimate, final freedom.

There exist two freedoms: the first—primordial freedom—and the last—final freedom. Between these two freedoms lies man's path, full of torments and sufferings, a path of inner division. Already Blessed Augustine, in his struggle against Pelagianism, taught of two freedoms: *libertas minor* and *libertas major*. The lower freedom was for him the primordial, first freedom, which is the freedom to choose good; it is bound up with the possibility of sin. The higher freedom was the last, final freedom—freedom in God, in the good. Blessed Augustine was an apologist for the second freedom, *libertas major*, and in the end arrived at a doctrine of predestination. Although semi-Pelagianism prevailed in church consciousness, Blessed

Augustine exerted an influence on Catholicism that was unfavorable to freedom. He gave sanction to the persecution and execution of heretics.

It remains beyond doubt: there is not one freedom but two, the first and the last—the freedom to choose good and evil, and the freedom in the good; or, irrational freedom and freedom in reason. Socrates knew only the second freedom, rational freedom. And the Gospel words—*"you shall know the Truth, and the Truth shall make you free"*—refer to the second freedom, freedom in Christ. When we say that man must liberate himself from lower elements, from the power of passions, must cease to be a slave to himself and to the surrounding world, we have in mind the second freedom. The highest attainment of freedom of spirit belongs to the second freedom. The freedom of the first Adam and the freedom of the second Adam, freedom in Christ—these are different freedoms.

The Truth makes man free, but man must freely accept the Truth; he cannot be led to it by force or compulsion. Christ gives man the final freedom, but man must freely accept Christ. "Thou didst desire man's free love, that he should follow Thee freely, enticed and captivated by Thee" (the words of the Grand Inquisitor). In this free acceptance of Christ lies all the dignity of the Christian, all the meaning of the act of faith, which is itself an act of freedom. The dignity of man, the dignity of his faith, presupposes the recognition of two freedoms: the freedom of good and evil, and the freedom in the good; the freedom to choose the Truth, and the freedom in the Truth.

Freedom cannot be identified with the good, with truth, with perfection. Freedom has its own autonomous nature; freedom is freedom, not good. And every confusion and identification of freedom with the good itself and with perfection is a denial of freedom, an acceptance of the paths of compulsion and violence. Compulsory good is no longer good; it degenerates into evil. But free good, which is the only true good, presupposes the freedom of evil. Herein lies the tragedy of freedom, which Dostoevsky investigated and grasped to the depths. Herein is hidden the mystery of Christianity.

A tragic dialectic unfolds. Good cannot be compulsory; one cannot compel the good. The freedom of good presupposes the freedom of evil. But the freedom of evil leads to the destruction of freedom itself, to degeneration into evil necessity. Yet the denial of the freedom of evil and the affirmation of an exclusive freedom of the good also leads to the denial of freedom, to the degeneration of freedom into good necessity. But good necessity is no longer good, for good presupposes freedom.

This tragic problem of freedom tormented Christian thought throughout its entire history. Bound up with it are the disputes of Blessed Augustine with Pelagianism, the teaching on the relation between freedom and grace, the disputes provoked by Jansenism, Luther's inclinations toward Augustinian predestination, and Calvin's grim doctrine, which seemed to deny all freedom. Christian thought was pressed between two dangers, two specters—evil freedom and good compulsion. Freedom perished either from the evil revealed within it, or from compulsion in the good. The pyres of the Inquisition were terrible witnesses to this tragedy of freedom, to the difficulty of resolving it even for Christian consciousness illumined by the light of Christ.

The denial of the first freedom—freedom in faith, in accepting the truth—must lead to the doctrine of predestination. The Truth itself brings one to it, without the participation of freedom. The Catholic world was tempted by freedom, inclined toward the denial of freedom—the denial of freedom of faith, freedom of conscience—toward violence in truth and good. The Orthodox world was not so tempted by this, but even in it the truth about freedom had not yet been fully revealed. For there exists not only freedom in the Truth, but also the Truth about freedom.

And should not the resolution of the age-old theme of freedom be sought in this: that Christ is not only the Truth that gives freedom, but also the Truth about freedom, the free Truth; that Christ is freedom, free love? Here formal and material elements intermingle in the understanding of freedom. The first freedom, as formal freedom, tends to be denied by those who already know the Truth and freedom in the Truth. The second freedom is understood as material freedom, freedom directed toward the Truth. Christian consciousness seems unwilling to adopt a formal standpoint and defend freedom of conscience, freedom of faith, as a formal right of man. Christianity knows the Truth that makes free. And this Truth is exclusive; it does not tolerate other truths alongside it, does not tolerate falsehood.

But is there not some error concealed in this seemingly impeccable course of thought? The error is hidden in the assumption that freedom of conscience, freedom of faith, freedom of good and evil can be defended exclusively from a formal standpoint. Freedom in Christianity is not a formal but a material Truth. The Truth of Christ itself is the Truth about freedom. Christianity is a religion of freedom. The very content of the Christian faith demands the recognition of freedom of faith, freedom of conscience—not only the second freedom, but also the first. Christianity is the overcoming of the tragedy of freedom and necessity. The grace of Christ is itself freedom, which is not destroyed by evil (the exclusivity of the first freedom) and is not destroyed by compulsion in the good (the exclusivity of the second freedom). Christianity is free love, and in the grace of free love divine freedom and human freedom are reconciled. The Truth of Christ casts its light back upon the first freedom as well, affirming it as an inseparable part of the Truth itself. The freedom of the human spirit, freedom of conscience, enters into the content of Christian Truth. All this had not yet been fully revealed by the old Christian consciousness, and least of all by the Catholic consciousness. Dostoevsky takes an enormous step forward in the work of revealing this Truth.

Dostoevsky allows man to walk the path of freely accepting that Truth which must make man finally free. But this path lies through darkness, through the abyss, through inner division, through tragedy. This path is neither straight nor smooth. Man wanders upon it, seduced by phantom visions, by deceptive light that lures him into still greater darkness. This path is long; it knows no line of direct ascent. It is a path of trials, an experiential path, a path of knowing good and evil through experience. This path could be shortened or made easier by limiting or taking away human freedom. But are those who come to God not by the path of freedom, not by experiential knowledge of all the ruinousness of evil, needed by God, dear to Him? Does not the meaning of the world process and the historical process lie in this divine thirst to encounter the free, answering love of man?

But man tarries in this movement of answering love toward God. He must first experience bitter disappointments and failures in love for corruptible and unworthy objects. The grace sent by God to man along the way is not coercive grace; it is only helping and alleviating grace. And every time the Christian world tried to turn the energy of this grace into an instrument of power and compulsion, it deviated toward anti-Christian, even antichristian paths. Dostoevsky perceived this Christian truth about the freedom of the human spirit with unprecedented acuteness.

The path of freedom is the path of the new man of the Christian world. Ancient man, or man of the ancient East, did not know this freedom; he was shackled in necessity, in the natural order, subject to fate. Only Christianity gave man this freedom—both the first freedom and the last freedom. In Christianity was revealed not only the freedom of the second Adam, of man born anew in the spirit, but also the freedom of the first Adam; not only the freedom of good, but also the freedom of evil. Greek thought admitted only rational freedom. Christianity also reveals the irrational principle of freedom. The irrational principle is disclosed in the content of life, and in it is hidden the mystery of freedom.

The Hellenic consciousness feared this irrational content as the boundless—*apeiron*—as matter; it fought against it with the principle of form, with the introduction of limit—*peras*. Therefore the Greek contemplated the world as enclosed by form, by limit; he did not see distant horizons. Man of the Christian world no longer fears infinity so much, the infinite content of life. Infinity is revealed to him; distant horizons open up. Bound up with this is a different attitude toward freedom in the man of the new Christian world than in ancient man. Freedom stands opposed to the exclusive dominion of the principle of form, of the limiting boundary. Freedom presupposes infinity. For the Greek this was exclusively chaos. For man of the Christian world, infinity is not only chaos but also freedom. Infinite human strivings are possible only in the Christian world.

Faust is a phenomenon of the Christian period of history; he is impossible in the ancient world. Faustian infinite strivings are most characteristic of Christian Europe. Only in the Christian world is Byron possible. Manfred, Cain, Don Juan could appear only in Christian Europe. This rebellious freedom, these stormy, restless strivings that know no limit, this irrational content of life—these are phenomena within the Christian world. The revolt of human personality against the world order, against fate, is an internally Christian phenomenon. Greek tragedy, like the heights of Greek philosophy, pointed to the inevitability of breaking through beyond the limits of the enclosed ancient world; they led to the new Christian world. But in Greek tragedy and Greek philosophy the Faustian soul was not yet revealed—this new, terrible freedom.

Rebellious freedom in Dostoevsky's heroes reaches the ultimate limits of intensity. Dostoevsky's heroes mark a new moment in human destiny within the Christian world, a later moment than Faust. Faust still stands in the middle of this path. Raskolnikov, Stavrogin, Kirillov, Ivan Karamazov stand already at the end of the path. After Faust the nineteenth century was still possible, which enthusiastically busied itself with draining swamps—which is where Faust ended up. After Dostoevsky's heroes opens an unknown twentieth century, a great unknown that reveals itself as a crisis of culture, as the end of an entire period of world history. The search for human freedom enters a new phase.

Freedom in Dostoevsky is not only a Christian phenomenon but also a phenomenon of the new spirit. It belongs to a new period within Christianity itself. This is the transition of Christianity from a period of exclusively transcendent understanding to a period of more immanent understanding. Man emerges from under external form, external law, and through suffering obtains inner light for himself. Everything passes into the ultimate depth of the human spirit. There a new world must be revealed. Transcendent consciousness, which objectified the Truth of Christianity externally, could not fully reveal Christian freedom. Christ must appear to man on his free paths as the final freedom, freedom in the Truth. He is revealed in the depths.

The first freedom is granted to man; it exhausts itself and passes into its opposite. Dostoevsky shows this tragic fate of freedom in the fate of his heroes: freedom passes into willfulness, into the rebellious self-assertion of man. Freedom becomes objectless, empty; it empties man. Thus the freedom of Stavrogin and Versilov is objectless and empty; the freedom of Svidrigailov and Fyodor Pavlovich Karamazov disintegrates personality. The freedom of Raskolnikov and Pyotr Verkhovensky leads to crime. The demonic freedom of Kirillov and Ivan Karamazov destroys man.

Freedom as willfulness destroys itself, passes into its opposite, disintegrates and destroys man. With inner, immanent inevitability such freedom leads to slavery, extinguishes the image of man. It is not external punishment that awaits man, not law laying its heavy hand upon man from without, but the divine principle revealing itself from within, immanently, strikes the human conscience; man is consumed by the scorching fire of God in that darkness and emptiness which he himself has chosen. Such is the fate of man, the fate of human freedom. And Dostoevsky reveals this fate with staggering brilliance.

Man must go the way of freedom. But freedom passes into slavery; freedom destroys man when, in the frenzy of his freedom, man refuses to know anything higher than himself. If there is nothing higher than man himself, then there is no man. If freedom has no content, no object, if there is no connection between human freedom and divine freedom, then there is no freedom. If everything is permitted to man, then human freedom passes into enslavement to oneself. And enslavement to oneself destroys man himself. The human image is upheld by a nature higher than itself. Human freedom attains its final expression in the higher freedom, freedom in the Truth. Such is the inexorable dialectic of freedom. It leads to the path of God-manhood. In God-manhood, human freedom is united with divine freedom, the human image with the divine image. By inner experience, by the inner living-through of freedom, the light of this Truth is won.

There can be no return to the exclusive dominion of external law, to life in necessity and compulsion. There remains only the restoration of freedom destroyed in the Truth—that is, in Christ. But Christ is not an external law, not an external order of life. His Kingdom is incommensurable with the kingdom of this world. And Dostoevsky wrathfully exposes all deviations of Christianity toward a religion of compulsion and violence. The light of the Truth, the good of final freedom, cannot be received from without. Christ Himself is the final freedom—not that objectless, rebellious, self-enclosed freedom which destroys man and extinguishes his image, but that freedom filled with content which affirms the image of man in eternity. To this Truth the fate of Raskolnikov and Stavrogin, of Kirillov and Ivan Karamazov, must bear witness. Wrongly directed freedom destroyed them. But this does not mean they should have been kept in compulsion, under the exclusive power of externally regulating law. Their destruction is luminous for us. Their tragedy is a hymn to freedom.

Dostoevsky had the idea that without the freedom of sin and evil, without the trial of freedom, world harmony cannot be accepted. He revolts against every compulsory harmony, whether Catholic, theocratic, or socialist. Human freedom cannot be received from a compulsory order as its gift. Human freedom must precede such an order and such a harmony. Through freedom must lie the path to order and harmony, to the worldwide union of people. Dostoevsky's dislike of Catholicism and socialism, as will be seen later, is connected with this impossibility of reconciling himself to compulsory order and harmony. He counterposes the freedom of the human spirit to both Catholicism and socialism. Herein lies the meaning of the revolt of the gentleman with the mocking and retrograde physiognomy.

Dostoevsky accepts neither the paradise in which freedom of spirit is not yet possible, nor the paradise in which it is no longer possible. Man had to pass through his fall from the compulsory world order; he had to conduct the world order through the freedom of his spirit. The faith on which Dostoevsky wished to organize social order must be a free faith. Upon the freedom of human conscience this faith rests. "Through the crucible of doubt my Hosanna has passed," Dostoevsky writes of himself. And he would wish that every faith be tempered in the crucible of doubt.

Dostoevsky was probably the most passionate defender of freedom of conscience the Christian world has ever known. "Their freedom of faith was dearer to Thee than anything," the Grand Inquisitor says to Christ. And he could say the same to Dostoevsky himself: "Thou didst desire man's free love." "Instead of the firm ancient law, man was henceforth to decide for himself with a free heart what is good and what is evil, having only Thy image before him for guidance." In these words of the Grand Inquisitor to Christ one senses the confession of faith of Dostoevsky himself. He rejects "miracle, mystery, and authority" as violence against human conscience, as the deprivation of man's freedom of spirit.

The three temptations with which the devil tempted Christ in the wilderness were directed against the freedom of the human spirit, the freedom of human conscience. Miracle must come from faith, not faith from miracle. Only then is faith free. No one violates human conscience in the appearance of Christ. The religion of Golgotha is a religion of freedom. The Son of God, who appeared in the world in "the form of a servant" and was crucified on the cross, torn apart by the world, appeals to the freedom of the human spirit. Nothing in the image of Christ coerces, nothing compels one to believe in Him as God. He was not power and might in the kingdom of this world. He preached a kingdom not of this world. Herein is hidden the fundamental mystery of Christianity, the mystery of freedom.

An extraordinary freedom of spirit is needed, a feat of free faith, a free discernment of "things unseen," to see one's God behind the servile image of Jesus. And when Peter said to Jesus, *"Thou art the Christ, the Son of the living God,"* he accomplished a feat of freedom. From the deep wellsprings of free human conscience came these words that determined the course of world history. And every person in the Christian world must repeat Peter's words from the depths of his own free spirit, his own free conscience. Herein lies all the dignity of the Christian. Not to Peter alone belongs this dignity of freedom of spirit, but to every Christian.

Dostoevsky believed that Christian freedom was better preserved in Eastern Orthodoxy than in Western Catholicism. Here there was exaggeration on his part. He was often unjust to the Catholic world, which cannot be considered wholly seized by an anti-Christian spirit. And he did not wish to see the deviations and failures in the Orthodox world. In Byzantinism, in imperial theocracy, there was no more Christian freedom than in papal theocracy. But he rightly noted a certain advantage of Orthodoxy over Catholicism on the question of freedom. Here the unfinished character of Orthodoxy helps. Yet in his religion of freedom of spirit he goes beyond the bounds of historical Orthodoxy and Catholicism; he is turned toward the future, and there is something prophetic in his revelations about freedom. But he is nonetheless flesh of the flesh and blood of the blood of Russian Orthodoxy.

Dostoevsky discovered that the antichristian principle is nothing other than the denial of freedom of spirit, violence against human conscience. And he investigates this principle to the depths. Christ is freedom; Antichrist is compulsion, violence, slavery of spirit. The antichristian principle assumes various guises in history—from Catholic theocracy to atheistic socialism and anarchism.

"Through the crucible of doubt" must pass Raskolnikov, Stavrogin, Kirillov, Versilov, Ivan Karamazov. From the depths of their spirit, from their free conscience, must resound the words of Peter: *"You are the Christ, the Son of the living God."* Dostoevsky sensed that their salvation lay in this. They must perish if they cannot find within themselves the free power of spirit to recognize in Jesus the Son of God. But if they do recognize Him, then the freedom of the underground man will pass over into the freedom of the sons of God.

Dostoevsky begins his investigation of freedom with the freedom of the "underground man." This freedom appears boundless. The underground man wishes to transgress the limits of human nature; he probes and tests these limits. If man is so free, is not everything permitted? Is not any crime whatsoever sanctioned in the name of higher ends, even parricide? Are not the Madonna ideal and the Sodom ideal of equal worth? Must not man strive to become a god himself? Is man not obliged to declare his self-will?

Dostoevsky sensed that in the freedom of the underground man lies the seed of death. Raskolnikov's freedom, transgressing the limits of human nature, engenders a consciousness of his own insignificance, impotence, and unfreedom. Stavrogin's freedom passes into complete powerlessness, indifference, into the exhaustion and extinction of personality. Kirillov's freedom, having desired to become God, ends in a terrible, fruitless destruction.

Perhaps Kirillov is the most important figure here. Kirillov recognizes self-will as a duty, as a sacred obligation. He must declare his self-will so that man may attain the highest state. And he is a pure man, detached from passions and impulses; there are traits in him of a graceless sanctity. But even the purest man, having rejected God and desired to become a god himself, is doomed to destruction. He already loses his freedom. He is possessed; he is in the power of spirits whose nature he himself does not know. And Kirillov presents to us the image of a quiet demonic possession and obsession, concentrated within himself. In the freedom of his spirit, morbid processes of degeneration have already occurred. He is the least spiritually free of men. On the paths of man-godhood, human freedom perishes, and man perishes. This is Dostoevsky's fundamental theme.

Thus freedom perishes in Dostoevsky's other divided heroes as well—in all who have gone astray on the paths of self-will. In Svidrigailov or Fyodor Pavlovich Karamazov, we encounter such a destruction of personality that there can be no talk of freedom at all. The unbridled, measureless freedom of sensuality makes a man its slave, deprives him of freedom of spirit. Dostoevsky is a great master at describing the degeneration and degradation of personality under the influence of possession by an evil passion or an evil idea. He investigates the ontological consequences of this possession. When unbridled freedom passes into possession, it perishes; it is no more. When a man begins to rage demonically, he is no longer free.

Is Versilov free—one of Dostoevsky's most noble images? His passion for Katerina Nikolaevna is a possession. This passion has been driven inward. It has exhausted him. In his relation to ideas, he knows no free volitional choice. Opposing ideas attract him. He wished to preserve his freedom and therefore lost it. He is divided. A divided man cannot be free. But everyone who does not perform the act of freely choosing the object of love is condemned to division.

The development of the theme of freedom reaches its summit in *The Brothers Karamazov*. The self-will and rebellion of Ivan Karamazov represent the pinnacle of the paths of graceless human freedom. Here it is revealed with extraordinary genius that freedom as self-will and human self-assertion must come to the denial not only of God, not only of the world and man, but also of freedom itself. Freedom destroys itself. And with this the dialectic of ideas reaches its conclusion.

Dostoevsky reveals that at the end of the path of dark, unillumined freedom lies in wait the final destruction of freedom, evil compulsion and evil necessity. The teaching of the Grand Inquisitor, like the teaching of Shigalyov, is born of self-will, of rebellion against God. Freedom passes into self-will; self-will passes into compulsion. This is a fateful process. Freedom of the human spirit, freedom of religious conscience, is denied by those who have walked the paths of self-will.

Those who have taken the paths of self-will and self-assertion, who have directed their freedom against God, cannot preserve freedom; they inevitably come to its violation. They must inevitably renounce the birthright of the human spirit, its primordial freedom; they betray freedom to the kingdom of necessity; they arrive at the greatest acts of violence. This is one of Dostoevsky's most brilliant insights.

"Starting from unlimited freedom," says Shigalyov, "I conclude with unlimited despotism." Such has always been the path of revolutionary freedom. Thus in the Great French Revolution the transition occurred from "unlimited freedom" to "unlimited despotism." Freedom as caprice and self-will, godless freedom, cannot but engender "unlimited despotism." Such freedom contains within itself the greatest violence. Such freedom carries no guarantees of freedom.

The rebellion of self-will leads to the denial of the Meaning of life, to the denial of Truth. Living Meaning and living Truth are replaced by the willful ordering of life, by the creation of human well-being in a social anthill. This process of the transformation of freedom into "unlimited despotism" occupies a very important place in Dostoevsky's worldview. In the revolutionary ideology of the left-wing Russian intelligentsia, outwardly so liberty-loving, he exposes the possibility of "unlimited despotism."

He saw many things first and saw further than others. He knew that the revolution, which he sensed in the subterranean, subsoil layer of Russia, would not lead to freedom; that a movement toward the final enslavement of the human spirit had begun. Already in the astonishing thoughts of the hero of *Notes from Underground*, what is definitively revealed in P. Verkhovensky, Shigalyov, and the Grand Inquisitor is outlined.

Like a nightmare, the idea haunted and pursued Dostoevsky that humanity, having betrayed the Truth of Christ, in its rebellion and self-will must come to the system of "unlimited despotism" of Shigalyov, P. Verkhovensky, and the Grand Inquisitor. This is one and the same system. In it is accomplished the renunciation of freedom of the human spirit in the name of human happiness. Social eudaemonism is opposed to freedom. Nothing remains but the compulsory organization of social happiness if there is no Truth.

Revolution is accomplished not in the name of freedom, but in the name of the same principles for which the fires of the Inquisition blazed—in the name of "thousands of millions of happy infants." Man could not bear the burden of freedom of spirit; he was terrified by the suffering path of freedom. And he renounces freedom, betrays freedom, flees from it to the compulsory ordering of human happiness. This denial of freedom began with its unlimited affirmation as self-will. Such is the fateful dialectic of freedom.

But if false freedom passes into "unlimited despotism," the complete destruction of freedom, then false equality must also lead to unheard-of inequality, to the tyrannical rule of a privileged minority over the majority. Dostoevsky always thought that revolutionary democracy and revolutionary socialism, possessed by the idea of absolute equality, at their ultimate limits must lead to the rule of a small handful over the rest of humanity. Such is Shigalyov's system, and such also is the system of the Grand Inquisitor. Dostoevsky returned to this thought more than once in *A Writer's Diary*. This thought bored into him, gave him no peace.

True freedom and true equality are possible only in Christ, on the God-manhood path. On the path of antichrist's self-will, on the path of man-godhood, only unheard-of tyranny awaits. Obsession with the idea of universal happiness, the universal union of people without God, contains within itself the terrible danger of man's destruction, the annihilation of the freedom of his spirit. Such are the vital consequences of freedom as self-will and rebellion.

But self-will and rebellion against the world's meaning close off for human consciousness access to the very idea of freedom. Freedom of spirit begins to be ideologically denied, as having become inaccessible to the mind that has torn itself away from eternal Meaning. The "Euclidean mind"—an expression Dostoevsky loved—is powerless to grasp the idea of freedom; it is inaccessible to it, as an utterly irrational mystery. The rebellion of the "Euclidean mind" against God is bound up with the denial of freedom, with incomprehension of freedom.

If there is no freedom as the ultimate mystery of world-creation, then this world with its torments and sufferings, with the tears of innocently tortured people, cannot be accepted. And the God who created such a terrible, ugly world cannot be accepted. Man in his self-will and rebellion, in the uprising of his "Euclidean mind," imagines that he could create a better world, in which there would be no such evil, no such sufferings, no tear of an innocent child. Such is the logic of rebellion against God in the name of love for the good.

God cannot be accepted because the world is so bad, because such untruth and injustice reign in the world. Freedom has led to this rebellion against God and against the world. And here again the fateful dialectic of freedom is revealed, the inner tragedy of freedom. It turns out that rebellious freedom has led to the denial of the very idea of freedom, to the impossibility of comprehending the mystery of the world and the mystery of God in the light of freedom.

For truly, one can accept God and accept the world, preserve faith in the Meaning of the world, if at the foundation of being lies the mystery of irrational freedom. Only then can the source of evil in the world be grasped and God be justified in the existence of this evil. There is so much evil and suffering in the world because at the foundation of the world lies freedom. And in freedom lies all the dignity of the world and the dignity of man.

Evil and suffering can be avoided only at the price of denying freedom. Then the world would be compulsorily good and happy. But it would be deprived of its likeness to God. For this God-likeness consists above all in freedom. That world which the rebellious "Euclidean mind" of Ivan Karamazov would create, unlike God's world full of evil and suffering, would be a good and happy world. But in it there would be no freedom; in it everything would be compulsorily rationalized.

From the very beginning, from the first day, it would be that happy social anthill, that compulsory harmony, which the "gentleman with a retrograde and mocking physiognomy" would wish to overthrow. There would be no tragedy of the world process, but there would be no Meaning either, bound up as it is with freedom. The "Euclidean mind" could construct a world exclusively on necessity, and this world would be exclusively a rational world. Everything irrational would be banished from it.

But God's world does not have a Meaning commensurate with the "Euclidean mind." This Meaning is for the "Euclidean mind" an impenetrable mystery. The "Euclidean mind" is limited to three dimensions. But the Meaning of God's world can be grasped if one passes into the fourth dimension. Freedom is a Truth of the fourth dimension; it is incomprehensible within the limits of three dimensions. The "Euclidean mind" is powerless to resolve the theme of freedom.

All who have declared self-will and rebellion come in Dostoevsky to the denial of freedom, because their consciousness narrows, enters into the limits of three dimensions, closes off other worlds to them. Rebellion began with freedom and ended with the attempt to construct a world on necessity alone. Dostoevsky investigates with astonishing dialectical power the fateful consequences of rebellious rationalism for human consciousness and of rebellious revolutionism for human life. Rebellion, having begun with unlimited freedom, inevitably arrives at unlimited dominion of necessity in thought and unlimited despotism in life.

Thus Dostoevsky writes his astonishing theodicy, which is also an anthropodicy. There is only one age-old objection against God—the existence of evil in the world. This theme is fundamental for Dostoevsky. And all his creative work is an answer to this objection.

I would formulate this answer paradoxically as follows: God exists precisely because there is evil and suffering in the world; the existence of evil is proof of God's existence. If the world were exclusively good and blessed, then God would not be needed; then the world would already be god. God exists because evil exists. This means that God exists because freedom exists.

Dostoevsky proves God's existence through freedom, the freedom of the human spirit. Those who in his work deny freedom of spirit also deny God, and vice versa. A world compulsorily good and blessed, a harmonious world by virtue of inexorable necessity, would be a godless world, would be a rational mechanism. And those who reject God and freedom of the human spirit strive to transform the world into such a rational mechanism, into such a compulsory harmony.

Dostoevsky treats the theme of freedom dynamically, not statically; his freedom is constantly in dialectical movement; inner contradictions unfold within it, and it passes from one phase to another. Therefore it is difficult for people of static thinking and static consciousness to understand Dostoevsky's great revelations about freedom. They demand "yes" or "no," whereas such answers cannot be given.

Freedom is the tragic fate of man and the world, the fate of God Himself, and it lies at the very center of being as its primordial mystery. We shall see that the dialectic of freedom reaches its completion in Dostoevsky in the "Legend of the Grand Inquisitor," in which all themes are concentrated and all threads are joined.

Chapter IV.
Evil

In Dostoevsky, the theme of evil and crime is bound up with the theme of freedom. Evil cannot be explained apart from freedom. Evil appears along the paths of freedom. Without this connection to freedom, there is no responsibility for evil. Without freedom, God would be answerable for evil. Dostoevsky understood more profoundly than anyone that evil is the child of freedom. But he also understood that without freedom there is no good. Good too is the child of freedom. Herein lies the mystery of life, the mystery of human destiny. Freedom is irrational, and therefore it can create both good and evil. Yet to reject freedom on the grounds that it may give birth to evil means to engender an even greater evil. For only free good is truly good, while compulsion and slavery that masquerade as virtue constitute the antichristian evil. Here we encounter nothing but riddles, antinomies, and mysteries. Dostoevsky not only places us before these riddles but does much to help us solve them.

Dostoevsky had a very distinctive, exceptional attitude toward evil—one that may lead many astray. It is necessary to understand fully how he posed and resolved the problem of evil. The path of freedom passes into self-will; self-will leads to evil; evil leads to crime. The problem of crime occupies a central place in Dostoevsky's creative work. He is not only an anthropologist but also a singular criminologist. His investigation of the limits and boundaries of human nature leads to an investigation of the nature of crime. In crime, man transgresses these limits and boundaries. Hence the extraordinary interest in crime. What fate befalls a person who transgresses the boundaries of the permissible? What transformations occur in his nature as a result? Dostoevsky reveals the ontological consequences of crime.

And so it turns out that freedom, having passed into self-will, leads to evil; evil leads to crime; and crime, with inner inevitability, leads to punishment. Punishment lies in wait for man in the very depths of his own nature. All his life Dostoevsky struggled against an external attitude toward evil. His novels and the articles in *A Writer's Diary* are filled with criminal cases. This strange interest in crime and punishment is determined by the fact that Dostoevsky's entire spiritual nature rebelled against the external explanation of evil and crime as products of the social environment, and the consequent denial of punishment. Dostoevsky felt hatred toward this positivist-humanitarian theory. He saw in it a denial of the depth of human nature, a denial of the freedom of the human spirit and of the responsibility bound up with it. If man is merely a passive reflex of the external social environment, if he is not a responsible being, then there is no man and there is no God, there is no freedom, no evil and no good.

Such a degradation of man, such a renunciation of one's birthright, aroused Dostoevsky's wrath. He could not speak calmly of this teaching, which so predominated in his time. He was prepared to stand for the most severe punishments as befitting the nature of responsible, free beings. Evil is rooted in the depths of human nature, in its irrational freedom, in its falling away from the divine nature; evil has an internal source. Those who advocate severe punishments have a deeper view of the nature of crime and of human nature in general than the humanistic denial of evil. In the name of human dignity, in the name of human freedom, Dostoevsky affirms the inevitability of punishment for every crime. This is required not by external law but by the very depths of man's free conscience. Man himself cannot reconcile himself to the notion that he is not responsible for evil and crime, that he is not a free being, not a spirit, but merely a reflection of the social environment.

In Dostoevsky's wrath, in his harshness, one hears a voice risen in defense of human dignity and human birthright. It is unworthy of a responsible, free being to lay down the burden of responsibility and place it upon external conditions, to feel oneself the plaything of those external conditions. All of Dostoevsky's creative work is an exposure of this slander against human nature. Evil is a sign that there exists an inner depth in man. Evil is connected with personality; only personality can create evil and answer for evil. An impersonal force cannot be responsible for evil, cannot be its primary source. Dostoevsky's attitude toward evil is bound up with his attitude toward personality, with his personalism. Irresponsible humanism denies evil because it denies personality. Dostoevsky struggled against humanism in the name of man. If man exists, if human personality exists in the dimension of depth, then evil has an internal source; it cannot be the result of accidental conditions in the external environment.

It accords with the highest dignity of man, with his divine sonship, to believe that the path of suffering redeems crime and burns away evil. This thought is very essential to Dostoevsky's anthropology: that only through suffering does man ascend. Suffering is an indicator of depth.

Dostoevsky's attitude toward evil was profoundly antinomian. The complexity of this attitude leads some to doubt whether it was Christian at all. One thing is beyond doubt: Dostoevsky's attitude toward evil was not a legalistic attitude. Dostoevsky wanted to know evil, and in this he was a gnostic. Evil is evil. The nature of evil is internal, metaphysical, not external, not social. Man, as a free being, is responsible for evil. Evil must be exposed in its nothingness and must be consumed by fire. And Dostoevsky ardently exposes and consumes evil. This is one side of his attitude toward evil.

But evil is also the path of man—his tragic path, the fate of a free being, an experience that can also enrich man and raise him to a higher level. In Dostoevsky there is also this other side in the attitude toward evil: an immanent apprehension of evil. This is how free sons, not slaves, experience evil. The immanent experience of evil exposes its nothingness; in this experience evil is consumed, and man comes to the light. But this truth is dangerous; it exists for those who are genuinely free and spiritually mature. From those who have not come of age it must be hidden. And for this reason Dostoevsky may seem a dangerous writer; he must be read in an atmosphere of spiritual liberation.

And yet it must be acknowledged that there is no writer who struggled so mightily against evil and darkness as Dostoevsky. The legalistic morality of the catechism cannot be an answer to the torment of those heroes of his who have embarked upon the path of evil. Evil is not punished externally; it has inescapable internal consequences. The punishment of law for crime is merely the internal fate of the criminal. Everything external is merely a sign of the internal. The torments of conscience are more terrible for a person than the external punishment of state law. And the man stricken by torments of conscience awaits punishment as a relief from his torment. The law of the state—that "cold monster"—is incommensurable with the human soul. In the investigation and trial of Mitya Karamazov, Dostoevsky exposes the untruth of state law. For Dostoevsky, the human soul has greater significance than all the kingdoms of the world. In this he was a Christian to the depths. But the soul itself seeks the sword of the state, places itself under its blows. Punishment is a moment in its internal path.

Only a slave or one who has not come of age can understand Dostoevsky's thesis about evil to mean that one should follow the path of evil in order to gain new experience and enrichment. One cannot construct from Dostoevsky an evolutionary theory of evil, according to which evil is merely a moment in the evolution of good. Such evolutionary optimism, defended by many theosophists, is utterly contrary to the tragic spirit of Dostoevsky. He was least of all an evolutionist for whom evil is a deficiency of good or a stage in the development of good. For him, evil was evil. Evil must be consumed in the fire of hell. And he conducts evil through this hellish fire. No childish games or cunning tricks with evil are possible. It is madness to think that a person can consciously embark upon the path of evil in order to obtain from it as much satisfaction as possible, and then advance even further in good. This is a thoroughly unworthy state of consciousness. Such reasoning lacks inner seriousness.

Let the tragic experience of evil enrich a person's spiritual world, sharpen his knowledge. Let there be no return to the more elementary state that preceded this experience of evil. Yet when one who follows the path of evil, who undergoes the experience of evil, begins to think that evil enriches him, that evil is merely a moment of good, a moment of his ascent—he falls still lower, disintegrates, and perishes; he cuts off his path to enrichment and ascent. Such a person can learn nothing from the experience of evil, can no longer rise. Only the exposure of evil, only great suffering from evil, can raise a person to a greater height. Self-satisfaction in evil is ruin itself. And Dostoevsky shows what torment the soul undergoes from evil and how the soul itself exposes evil within itself.

Evil is the tragic path of man, the fate of man, the trial of human freedom. But evil is not a necessary moment in the evolution of good. Evil is antinomian. The optimistic-evolutionary understanding of evil is a rational resolution of this antinomy. One can be enriched from the experience of evil, attain a greater acuity of consciousness, but for this one must pass through suffering, experience the horror of perdition, expose evil, cast it into the fire of hell, and redeem one's guilt. Evil is bound up with suffering and must lead to redemption. Dostoevsky believes in the redeeming and regenerating power of suffering. For him, life is above all the redemption of guilt through suffering. Therefore freedom is inevitably bound up with redemption. Freedom led man onto the path of evil. Evil was the trial of freedom. Evil itself must lead to redemption. In the evil engendered by freedom, freedom perishes, passes into its opposite. Redemption restores man's freedom, returns freedom to him. Therefore Christ the Redeemer is freedom itself.

In all his novels Dostoevsky leads man through this spiritual process—through freedom, evil, and redemption. The Elder Zosima and Alyosha are portrayed by him as people who have known evil and have arrived at the highest state. In Alyosha there is the Karamazov element; both his brother Ivan and Grushenka discern it in him. He himself senses it within. According to Dostoevsky's design, Alyosha is to be a man who has passed through the trial of freedom. This is how Dostoevsky understood the fate of man.

The problem of crime is the problem of whether all is permitted. Is all permitted? This theme always tormented Dostoevsky; it presented itself to him in ever new forms. On this theme *Crime and Punishment* was written, as well as, to a significant degree, *Demons* and *The Brothers Karamazov*. This theme is posed through the trial of human freedom. When man set out on the path of freedom, the question arose before him: do moral boundaries to his nature exist, and can he dare everything? Freedom passing into self-will no longer wishes to recognize any sanctities, any limitations. If there is no God, if man himself is god, then all is permitted. And so man tests his powers, his might, his calling to become a man-god. Man becomes possessed by some "idea," and in this possession his freedom already begins to fade; he becomes the slave of some alien force. This process is brilliantly depicted by Dostoevsky.

He who in his self-will knows no boundaries to his freedom loses that freedom; he becomes possessed by an "idea" that enslaves him. Such is Raskolnikov. He does not at all give the impression of a free man. He is a maniac, possessed by a false "idea." He has no moral autonomy, for moral autonomy is achieved through self-purification and self-liberation. What is Raskolnikov's "idea"? In Dostoevsky, after all, everyone has his own "idea." Raskolnikov tests the boundaries of his own nature, of human nature in general. He considers himself as belonging to the chosen part of humanity—not to ordinary people, but to remarkable people called to benefit humanity. He thinks that everything is permitted and wants to test his power.

And so the moral problem facing a person with such a consciousness is simplified by Dostoevsky to an elementary theorem. Can an extraordinary man, called to serve humanity, kill the most insignificant and most hideous human creature—a vile old pawnbroker woman who causes people nothing but harm—in order thereby to open for himself a path to benefiting humanity in the future? Is this permitted?

And with striking power it is revealed in *Crime and Punishment* that this is not permitted, that such a person spiritually kills himself. Here, in immanently lived experience, it is shown that not everything is permitted, because human nature is created in the image and likeness of God, and therefore every human being has unconditional significance. The willful murder of even the least of people, even the most malignant of people, is not sanctioned by the spiritual nature of man. When man in his self-will destroys another person, he destroys himself as well; he ceases to be human, loses his human image, and his personality begins to disintegrate. No "idea," no "lofty" goals can justify a criminal attitude toward even the least of one's neighbors. The "neighbor" is more precious than the "distant one"; every human life, every human soul is worth more than the benefiting of future humanity, more than abstract "ideas." Such is Christian consciousness. And this is what Dostoevsky reveals.

The man who fancied himself a Napoleon, a great man, a man-god, having transgressed the boundaries permitted by the God-like human nature, falls low and is convinced that he is not a superman but a powerless, base, trembling creature. Raskolnikov becomes conscious of his utter impotence, his insignificance. The trial of the limits of his freedom and his power led to terrible results. Together with the insignificant and malignant old woman, Raskolnikov destroyed himself. After the "crime," which was a pure experiment, he lost his freedom and was crushed by his impotence. He no longer has a proud consciousness. He understood that it is easy to kill a person, that this experiment is not so difficult—but that it gives no power, that it deprives a person of spiritual strength.

Nothing "great," "extraordinary," or world-significant came of Raskolnikov's killing the pawnbroker; he was crushed by the insignificance of what had occurred. The eternal law entered into its rights, and he fell under its power. Christ came not to abolish the law but to fulfill it. And the freedom that the New Testament brings does not rebel against the Old Testament but only reveals a still higher world. And Raskolnikov must fall under the action of the immutable Old Testament law. This is not how those acted who were truly great and gifted with genius, who accomplished great deeds for all humanity. They did not consider themselves supermen to whom all was permitted; they sacrificially served the superhuman and therefore alone could give much to the human.

Raskolnikov is above all a divided, reflecting man; his freedom is already afflicted with an internal disease. The truly great are not like this; in them there is wholeness. Dostoevsky exposes the falseness of pretensions to superhumanity. It turns out that the false idea of superhumanity destroys the human being, that the pretension to boundless strength reveals weakness and impotence. All these modern strivings toward superhuman power are paltry and pitiful; they end in man's being cast down into inhuman weakness. And the nature of moral and religious conscience proves eternal. The torment of conscience not only exposes crime but also exposes man's impotence in his false pretensions to power. Raskolnikov's torments of conscience not only reveal that he transgressed the limit of the permissible but also expose his weakness and insignificance.

The theme of Raskolnikov already signifies a crisis of humanism, the end of humanist morality, the destruction of man through man's own self-assertion. The emergence of the dream of the superman and superhumanity, of a higher human morality, signifies that humanism has been exhausted and has ended. For Raskolnikov, humanity no longer exists; his relation to his neighbor is cruel and merciless. The human being—the living, suffering, concrete human creature—must be sacrificed to a superhuman "idea." In the name of the "distant one," of the inhuman "distant one," one may do as one pleases with the "neighbor," with the human being.

Dostoevsky himself professes the religion of love for the "neighbor," and he exposes the lie of the religion of love for the "distant one," for the inhuman, the superhuman. There is a "distant one" who commanded love for the "neighbor." This is God. But the idea of God is the only superhuman idea that does not annihilate man, that does not turn man into a mere means and instrument. God reveals Himself through His Son. And His Son is perfect God and perfect man, the God-Man, in whom the divine and the human are perfectly united. Every other superhuman idea annihilates man, turns man into a means and instrument. The idea of the man-god brings death to man. This can be seen in the example of Nietzsche. Equally fatal for humanity is the idea of the inhuman collective in Marx, in the religion of socialism.

Dostoevsky investigates the fateful consequences of man's possession by the idea of man-godhood in its various forms, both individualistic and collectivistic. Here the kingdom of humanity ends; here there will be no mercy for man. Humanity was still a reflection of the Christian truth about man. The final betrayal of this truth abolishes the humane treatment of human beings. In the name of the greatness of the superman, in the name of the happiness of a coming, distant humanity, in the name of world revolution, in the name of the unlimited freedom of one or the unlimited equality of all, one may torment or put to death any human being, any number of people, turn any human being into a mere means for a great "idea," a great goal.

Everything is permitted in the name of the unlimited freedom of the superman (extreme individualism) or in the name of the unlimited equality of humanity (extreme collectivism). Human self-will is granted the right to evaluate human lives as it sees fit and to dispose of them. Human life does not belong to God, and the final judgment over people does not belong to God. This is taken upon himself by the man who has imagined himself the possessor of a superhuman "idea." And his judgment is merciless, godless, and inhuman. Dostoevsky investigates to the depths the fateful paths of this human self-will, in its individualistic and collectivistic forms, and exposes their seductive lie.

Raskolnikov is one of those possessed by such a false idea. He himself, by his own self-will and caprice, decides the question of whether one may kill even the least of human beings in the name of his "idea." But the decision of this question belongs not to man but to God. God is the only supreme "idea." And whoever does not bow before the Higher Will in deciding this question destroys his neighbors and himself. This is the meaning of *Crime and Punishment*.

The paths of human self-will that lead to crime Dostoevsky investigates further and more deeply in *The Devils*. There the fateful consequences of possession by both a godless individualistic idea and a godless collectivistic idea are revealed. Pyotr Verkhovensky loses his human image through possession by a false idea. The destruction of the human being has gone far beyond what we saw in Raskolnikov. Pyotr Verkhovensky is capable of anything; he considers everything permitted in the name of his "idea." For him, human beings no longer exist, and he himself is no longer human. We are already leaving the human kingdom and entering some eerie, inhuman element.

Possession by the godless idea of revolutionary socialism leads, in its final results, to inhumanity. A moral idiotization of human nature takes place; all criteria of good and evil are lost. An eerie atmosphere forms, saturated with blood and murder. The murder of Shatov produces a shattering impression. There is something prophetic, something visionary, in the picture that unfolds in *The Devils*. Dostoevsky was the first to perceive the inevitable consequences of a certain kind of ideas.

He saw more deeply than Vladimir Solovyov, who made witticisms about Russian nihilists, attributing to them the formula: man descended from the ape, therefore let us love one another. No—if man is not the image and likeness of God but the image and likeness of the ape, then people will not love one another; they will annihilate one another; they will permit themselves any murder and any cruelty. Then everything is permitted.

Dostoevsky showed the degeneration and perversion of the very "idea" itself, of the very ultimate goal that at first seemed lofty and seductive. The "idea" itself is ugly, senseless, and inhuman; in it, freedom passes over into unlimited despotism, equality into terrible inequality, the deification of man into the annihilation of human nature. In Pyotr Verkhovensky—one of Dostoevsky's most hideous figures—human conscience, which still existed in Raskolnikov, has been completely destroyed. He is no longer capable of repentance; the demonic frenzy has gone too far. Therefore he belongs to those figures in Dostoevsky who have no further human destiny, who fall out of the human kingdom into nonbeing. He is straw. Such are Svidrigailov, Fyodor Pavlovich Karamazov, Smerdyakov, the eternal husband. Raskolnikov, Stavrogin, Kirillov, Versilov, and Ivan Karamazov, by contrast, have a future—even if empirically they perish—they still have a human destiny.

Dostoevsky investigates and reveals the torments of conscience and repentance at such depths as had never before been seen; he discovers the will to crime in the very last depths of man, in man's secret thoughts. The torments of conscience consume the human soul even when a person has committed no visible crimes. A person repents, accuses himself, even though the will to crime has not passed into any actions. Not only the law of the state but also the moral judgment of public opinion does not reach the very depths of human criminality. A person knows more terrible things about himself and considers himself deserving of more severe punishment. Human conscience is more merciless than the cold law of the state; it demands more of a person.

We kill our neighbors not only when we end their physical life with a firearm or cold steel. A secret thought—not always reaching human consciousness—directed toward the negation of our neighbor's being is already murder in spirit, and a person is responsible for it. All hatred is already murder. And we are all murderers and criminals, even if the law of the state and public opinion consider us in this respect irreproachable and deserving of no punishment. But how many murderous currents we emit from the depths of our souls, from the sphere of the subconscious! How often is our will directed toward the diminishment and annihilation of the lives of our neighbors! Many of us, in the secret places of the soul, have wished death upon our neighbor. Crime begins in these secret thoughts and wishes.

In Dostoevsky, the work of conscience becomes extraordinarily deepened and refined; it exposes crime that escapes every state and human judgment. Ivan Karamazov did not kill his father Fyodor Pavlovich. Smerdyakov killed him. But Ivan Karamazov condemns himself for the crime of patricide; the torments of conscience drive him to madness. He reaches the ultimate limits of the splitting of personality. His inner evil appears to him as his other "I" and torments him. In his secret thoughts, in the sphere of the subconscious, Ivan wished for the death of his father Fyodor Pavlovich, an evil and hideous man. And he was constantly talking about how "everything is permitted." He seduced Smerdyakov, supported his criminal will, strengthened it. He is the spiritual perpetrator of the patricide. Smerdyakov is his second, lower "I."

Neither the judgment of the state nor the judgment of public opinion suspects or accuses Ivan of anything; it does not reach to this depth. But he himself experiences torments of conscience from which his soul burns in hellfire, from which his mind grows clouded. False, godless "ideas" led him to secret thoughts that justify patricide. And if he is a person who will still have his own destiny, he must pass through fiery repentance, through madness.

Mitya Karamazov, too, did not kill his father and fell victim to an unjust human judgment. But he said: "Why does such a man live?" And by this he committed patricide in the depths of his spirit. The unjust, undeserved punishment of the cold law he accepts as expiation for his guilt.

The entire psychology of patricide in *The Brothers Karamazov* has a very deep, hidden, symbolic meaning. The path of man's godless self-will must lead to patricide, to the denial of fatherhood. Revolution, after all, is always patricide. The depiction of the relations between Ivan Karamazov and his other, lower "I"—Smerdyakov—belongs to the most brilliant pages in Dostoevsky. The path of self-will, the path that rejects reverence for the superhuman, must lead to the rising up of the figure of Smerdyakov. Smerdyakov is the terrible retribution that lies in wait for man. The terrible, hideous caricature of Smerdyakov stands at the end of these strivings toward man-godhood. Smerdyakov will triumph on this path. Ivan, however, must go mad.

We see the same deep exposure of crime in secret thoughts—even if it was only connivance—in Stavrogin's relation to the death of his wife, the Lame Woman. Fedka the Convict, the perpetrator of the Lame Woman's death, considers himself seduced by Stavrogin, as though he were his agent. And Stavrogin feels his guilt. This is the depth at which Dostoevsky poses the problem of evil and crime.

"Without a 'higher idea,' neither man nor nation can exist. And there is only one higher idea on earth, namely the idea of the immortality of the human soul, for all other 'higher ideas' of life by which man may live flow from it alone." "Suicide, upon the loss of the idea of immortality, becomes an absolute and inevitable necessity for every person who has risen even slightly above the level of cattle." "The idea of immortality is life itself, living life, its final formula and the chief source of truth and right consciousness for humanity." Thus wrote Dostoevsky in *Diary of a Writer* about immortality.

Dostoevsky had a thought central to him: that if there is no immortality, then everything is permitted. The problem of evil and the problem of crime were for him bound up with the problem of immortality. How should we understand this connection? Dostoevsky's thought does not mean that he had an elementary, simplified, and utilitarian formulation of the problem of evil and crime. He did not mean to say that for evil and crime a person will receive punishment in eternal life, and for good a reward. Such primitive celestial utilitarianism was alien to him.

Dostoevsky meant to say that every person and his life have unconditional significance only if he is an immortal being. The denial of human immortality was for him equivalent to the denial of man. Either man is an immortal spirit with an eternal destiny, or he is a transient empirical phenomenon, a passive product of the natural and social environment. In the second case, man has no unconditional value. Evil and crime do not exist.

Dostoevsky defends the immortal soul of man. The immortal soul, which means also the free soul, has eternal, unconditional value. But it is also a responsible soul. Recognition of the existence of inner evil and responsibility for crimes means recognition of the genuine being of the human person. Evil is bound up with personal being, with human selfhood. But personal being is immortal being. The destruction of immortal personal being is evil. The affirmation of immortal personal being is good. The denial of immortality is the denial that good and evil exist. Everything is permitted if man is not an immortal and free personal being. Then man has no unconditional value. Then man is not responsible for evil.

At the center of Dostoevsky's moral worldview stands the recognition of the absolute significance of every human being. The life and destiny of even the least of human beings has absolute significance before the face of eternity. This is eternal life and eternal destiny. And therefore no human being can be crushed with impunity. In every human being one must honor the image and likeness of God. Even the most fallen human being preserves the image and likeness of God. This is Dostoevsky's moral pathos.

Not only the "distant one"—the supreme "idea"—not only "extraordinary" people like Raskolnikov, Stavrogin, and Ivan Karamazov have unconditional significance, but also the "neighbor," be it Marmeladov, Lebyadkin, Snegirev, or the loathsome old moneylender woman—they too have unconditional significance. A person who kills another person kills himself, denies immortality and eternity in the other and in himself. Such is Dostoevsky's moral dialectic—irresistible and purely Christian. It is not utilitarian fear of punishment that should restrain one from crimes and murder, but one's own immortal nature, which is denied by crime and murder. Human conscience is the expression of this immortal nature.

Dostoevsky had a twofold relation to suffering. And this duality, not immediately comprehensible, justifies the contradictory assessments of Dostoevsky as the most compassionate and the most cruel of writers. Dostoevsky's creative work is permeated with boundless compassion for human beings. Dostoevsky teaches pity and compassion. In this he has no equal. No one was so wounded by the infinite suffering of humanity. Dostoevsky's heart eternally oozed blood. He was given to know hard labor, to live among convicts, and all his life he interceded for man before God.

The suffering of innocent children struck and wounded his conscience more than anything else. And the justification of a child's tear became for him the possibility of theodicy. He understood to the depths the rebellion against a world order purchased at the price of terrible sufferings, of the tears of innocently tormented children. He proceeded entirely from boundless compassion.

And through the lips of Alyosha he answered Ivan's question—whether he would consent "to erect the edifice of human destiny with the goal of ultimately making people happy, of giving them peace and rest at last"—if "for this it was necessary and inevitable to torture just one tiny creature, that same little child beating its breast with its little fist, and to found that edifice upon its unavenged tears": *"No, I would not consent."*

And all his life Dostoevsky asked, as in Mitya's dream: "Why do the burned-out mothers stand there, why are the people poor, why is the child poor, why is the steppe bare, why do they not embrace and kiss, why do they not sing joyful songs, why have they turned so black from black misfortune, why do they not feed the child?"

Yet Dostoevsky can least of all be called a sentimental, saccharine, and enervating humanist. He preached not only compassion but also suffering. He called people to suffering and believed in the redemptive power of suffering. Man is a responsible being. And human suffering is not innocent suffering. Suffering is bound up with evil. Evil is bound up with freedom. Therefore freedom leads to suffering. The path of freedom is the path of suffering. And there is always the temptation to deliver man from suffering by depriving him of freedom.

Dostoevsky is an apologist for freedom. Therefore he proposes that man accept suffering as its inevitable consequence. Dostoevsky's cruelty is bound up with this acceptance of freedom to the end. To Dostoevsky himself are applicable the words of the Grand Inquisitor: *"You took all that was exceptional, enigmatic, and indefinite, You took all that was beyond the strength of people, and therefore You acted as if You did not love them at all."* This "exceptional, enigmatic, and indefinite" is bound up with the irrational freedom of man.

In suffering Dostoevsky saw the sign of man's higher dignity, the sign of a free being. Suffering is the consequence of evil. But in suffering, evil is burned away. In his creative works, Dostoevsky leads man through purgatory and hell. He leads him to the threshold of paradise. But paradise is not revealed with the same force as hell.

The path of freedom has led man onto the paths of evil. And the path of evil splits man in two. Dostoevsky is a genius in depicting this splitting. Here he has made genuine discoveries that astonish psychologists and psychiatrists. More was revealed to the great artist, and revealed earlier, than to scientists. Boundless and empty freedom—freedom that has passed into self-will, graceless and godless freedom—cannot perform an act of choice; it is pulled in opposite directions. Therefore man is split; two "I"s form within him; personality is fractured.

All of Dostoevsky's heroes are such split, fractured people—Raskolnikov, Stavrogin, Versilov, Ivan Karamazov. They have lost the integrity of personality; they lead, as it were, a double life. At the limit of splitting, man's other "I," his inner evil, must separate out and become personified as the devil. This limit of splitting Dostoevsky reveals with genius in Ivan Karamazov's nightmare, in his conversation with the devil.

Ivan says to the devil: "You are the embodiment of myself, though only of one side of me... of my thoughts and feelings, but only the most loathsome and stupid ones." "You are I, I myself, only with a different mug." "You are not yourself; you are I, you are I and nothing more. You are rubbish; you are my fantasy."

The devil in Dostoevsky is no longer the seductive and beautiful demon who appeared "in a crimson glow, thundering and flashing, with fiery wings." He is a gray and vulgar gentleman with a lackey's soul who longs to become incarnate in "a fat merchant's wife of seventeen stone." He is the spirit of nonbeing lying in wait for man. The ultimate limit of evil is banality, nothingness, and nonbeing. The evil in Ivan Karamazov is the Smerdyakov element. Common sense prevented the devil from accepting Christ and exclaiming "Hosanna." Ivan Karamazov's "Euclidean mind" is closely akin to this common sense; the arguments of the "Euclidean mind" turn out to be arguments similar to those of the devil.

This devil exists in all of Dostoevsky's split people, though less manifest in them than in Ivan. The second "I" of the split person is the spirit of nonbeing, the destruction of the being of their personality. In this second "I" is revealed empty, contentless freedom—the freedom of nonbeing. The "Sodom ideal" is a "phantom of life," the temptation of nonbeing. And Svidrigailov, who has definitively given himself over to the Sodom ideal, turns into a complete phantom. He no longer exists as a personality. The immanent nothingness of evil is exposed.

Salvation from splitting lies only in the second, grace-filled freedom—freedom in Truth, freedom in Christ. For the splitting to cease and the nightmare of the devil to vanish, one must perform the final choice, the choice of genuine being. And love in Dostoevsky passes through the same splitting. In it the same principles are revealed.

Chapter V.
Love

All of Dostoevsky's creative work is saturated with burning, passionate love. Everything unfolds in an atmosphere of intense passion. He discovers within the Russian elemental nature a principle that is passionate and voluptuous. There is nothing comparable in other Russian writers. That elemental folk spirit which revealed itself in our Khlysty movement, Dostoevsky also uncovers in our educated class. This is a Dionysian element. Love in Dostoevsky is exclusively Dionysian. It torments the human being. The path of the person in Dostoevsky is a path of suffering. Love in his work consists of volcanic eruptions, dynamite explosions of the passionate nature of man. This love knows no law and knows no form. In it, the depths of human nature are revealed. In it there is the same passionate dynamism as in everything else in Dostoevsky. It is a consuming fire and a fiery movement. Then this fire turns to icy cold. Sometimes a lover appears to us as an extinguished volcano.

Russian literature does not possess such beautiful images of love as the literature of Western Europe. We have nothing resembling the love of the troubadours, the love of Tristan and Isolde, Dante and Beatrice, Romeo and Juliet. The love between man and woman, the amorous cult of woman—this is a beautiful flower of the Christian culture of Europe. We did not experience chivalry; we had no troubadours. In this lies a deficiency of our spirit. There is something heavy and tormenting in Russian love, something unilluminated and often grotesque. We had no genuine romanticism in love. Romanticism is a phenomenon of Western Europe.

Love occupies an enormous place in Dostoevsky's creative work. But this place is not independent. Love is not self-sufficient; it does not have its own image; it is merely a revelation of the tragic path of the human being, a testing of human freedom. Here love occupies an entirely different place than Tatyana's love in Pushkin or Anna Karenina's love in Tolstoy. Here the feminine principle occupies an entirely different position. Woman does not hold an independent place in Dostoevsky's creative work. Dostoevsky's anthropology is exclusively masculine anthropology. We shall see that woman interests Dostoevsky solely as a moment in man's fate, in the path of the human being. The human soul is first and foremost the masculine spirit. The feminine principle is merely an internal theme in the tragedy of the masculine spirit, an internal temptation.

What images of love has Dostoevsky left us? Myshkin's and Rogozhin's love for Nastasya Filippovna, Mitya Karamazov's love for Grushenka and Versilov's for Katerina Nikolaevna, Stavrogin's love for many women. Nowhere is there a beautiful image of love; nowhere is there a feminine image possessing independent significance. Always it is the tragic fate of the man that torments. Woman is merely the internal masculine tragedy.

Dostoevsky reveals the inescapable tragic nature of love, the impossibility of realizing love, its unattainability on the paths of life's ordering. Love in his work is just as murderous as in Tyutchev:

Oh, how murderously we love, How in the blind fury of passions We most surely destroy What is dearest to our heart.

In Dostoevsky there is neither the charm of love nor the seemliness of family life. He takes the human being at that moment of his fate when all the foundations of life have already been shaken. He does not reveal to us the higher love that leads to genuine union and fusion. The mystery of marriage is not realized. Love is exclusively a tragedy of the human being, a splitting of the human being. Love is a principle that is dynamic in the highest degree, one that heats the entire atmosphere to incandescence and summons forth whirlwinds, yet love is not an achievement—nothing is achieved in it. It leads to destruction.

Dostoevsky reveals love as a manifestation of human self-will. Love splits and divides human nature. Therefore it is never a union and never leads to union. In Dostoevsky's creative work there is only one theme—the tragic fate of the human being, the fate of human freedom. Love is merely one of the moments in this fate. But the fate of the human being is only the fate of Raskolnikov, Stavrogin, Kirillov, Myshkin, Versilov, Ivan, Dmitri, and Alyosha Karamazov. It is not the fate of Nastasya Filippovna, Aglaya, Liza, Elizaveta Nikolaevna, Grushenka, or Katerina Nikolaevna. This is masculine fate. Woman is merely a difficulty encountered along this path; she does not interest Dostoevsky in herself, but only as an internal phenomenon of masculine fate.

In Dostoevsky one cannot find a cult of the Eternal Feminine. And that special relationship he had to the mother—the moist earth—and to the Mother of God is in no way connected with his feminine images or with his depiction of love. Only in the image of the Lame Woman does something seem to be revealed. But even this is usually too greatly exaggerated. Dostoevsky is interested in Stavrogin, not in the Lame Woman. She was merely his fate. In his creative work Dostoevsky reveals the tragic path of his own masculine spirit, which for him was the path of the human being. Woman played a great role on this path. But woman is merely the temptation and passion of the man.

In Dostoevsky there is nothing comparable to Tolstoy's penetration into the feminine images of Anna Karenina or Natasha. Anna Karenina not only has an independent life; she is the main, central figure. Nastasya Filippovna and Grushenka are merely elemental forces in which men's fates are submerged; they do not have their own fate. Dostoevsky is interested in the fate of Myshkin and Rogozhin, while Nastasya Filippovna is that in which this fate is realized. He is unable to live with Nastasya Filippovna the way Tolstoy lived with Anna Karenina. The infernal quality of women interests Dostoevsky only as an element that awakens masculine passion and splits the personality of the man. The man turns out to be enclosed within himself; he does not go out of himself into another, feminine existence. Woman is merely the settling of masculine accounts with oneself, merely the resolution of one's own masculine, human theme.

The fate of the human being for Dostoevsky is the fate of personality, of the personal principle in man. But the personal principle is preeminently the masculine principle. This is why Dostoevsky shows such exclusive interest in the masculine soul and so little interest in the feminine soul. One cannot trace the fate of human personality through the history of the feminine soul. And therefore woman can be interesting only as the element and atmosphere in which the fate of the man unfolds, the fate of personality par excellence. The man in Dostoevsky is bound to woman by passion. But this remains, as it were, his affair with himself, with his own passionate nature. He never unites with the woman. And perhaps this is why the feminine nature in Dostoevsky is so hysterical, so lacerated—because it is condemned to non-union with the masculine nature.

Dostoevsky affirms the inescapable tragic character of love. He never reveals to us the androgynous human nature. In his work the human being remains a tragically divided man who does not possess his own Sophia, his own Virgin. Dostoevsky was insufficiently aware that human nature is androgynous, as was revealed to the great mystics—to Jakob Böhme and others. Deep in him was only the posing of the theme that woman is the fate of man. But he himself remained separated from the feminine nature and came to know only division to its depths. For him the human being is man, not androgyne.

In the tragedy of the masculine spirit, woman signifies division. Sexual love, passion, speaks of the loss of the wholeness of human nature. Therefore passion is not chaste. Chastity is wholeness. Depravity is torn-apartness. Dostoevsky leads the human being through division in everything. And in his work love is divided into two principles. His characters usually love two women. Double love and doubling in love are depicted by him with extraordinary power. He reveals two principles in love, two elements, two abysses into which the human being falls—the abyss of voluptuousness and the abyss of compassion. Love in Dostoevsky always reaches the limit; it proceeds from frenzied voluptuousness and from frenzied compassion.

Dostoevsky was interested only in revealing these ultimate elements of love. He was not interested in measure in love. After all, he conducted experiments on human nature and wanted to investigate its depths by placing the human being in exceptional conditions. In Dostoevsky love always splits; the object of love splits. There is no unified, integral love. And so it must be on the paths of human self-will. In this splitting, an essential damage to personality occurs. Human personality is threatened with the loss of the wholeness of its image. Both love-as-voluptuousness and love-as-compassion, knowing no measure, subordinated to nothing higher, equally burn up and reduce the human being to ashes. In the depths of compassion itself Dostoevsky discovers a peculiar voluptuousness.

The passion of the non-integral, divided human being passes into frenzy, and the division, the torn-apartness, is not thereby overcome. He remains within himself, in his division. He brings this division of his into love. Love leads to destruction at both its opposite poles. Union, wholeness, victory over division is never achieved. Neither boundless voluptuousness nor boundless compassion unites one with the beloved. The human being remains alone, left to himself in his polar passions; he only exhausts his strength.

Love in Dostoevsky is almost always demonic; it gives rise to demonic frenzy; it heats the surrounding atmosphere to white heat. Not only do the lovers begin to go mad, but everyone around them begins to go mad as well. Versilov's frenzied love for Katerina Nikolaevna creates an atmosphere of madness; it holds everyone in the greatest tension. The currents of love connecting Myshkin, Rogozhin, Nastasya Filippovna, and Aglaya heat the entire atmosphere to incandescence. The love of Stavrogin and Liza gives rise to demonic whirlwinds. The love of Mitya Karamazov, Ivan, Grushenka, and Katerina Ivanovna leads to crime and drives people mad. Never and nowhere does love find peace for itself, never does it lead to the joy of union. There is no ray of light in love. Everywhere there is revealed trouble in love, a dark and destructive principle, the torment of love. Love does not overcome division but deepens it still further.

Two women, like two suffering elements, always wage a merciless struggle over love, destroying themselves and others. Thus Nastasya Filippovna and Aglaya clash in *The Idiot*, Grushenka and Katerina Ivanovna in *The Brothers Karamazov*. There is something that knows no mercy in the rivalry and struggle of these women. The same atmosphere of rivalry and struggle of feminine passions exists in *Demons* and in *The Adolescent*, though in less pronounced form.

The masculine nature is divided. The feminine nature is not illumined; in it there is an attractive abyss, but there is never the image of a blessed mother nor the image of a blessed virgin. The fault here lies with the masculine principle. It has torn itself away from the feminine principle, from the mother-earth, from its own virginity—that is, its own chastity and wholeness—and has gone the way of wandering and doubling. The masculine principle proves powerless before the feminine principle. Stavrogin is powerless before Liza and the Lame Woman, Versilov is powerless before Katerina Nikolaevna, Myshkin is powerless before Nastasya Filippovna and Aglaya, Mitya Karamazov is powerless before Grushenka and Katerina Ivanovna. Men and women remain tragically separated and torment each other. The man is powerless to master the woman; he does not take the feminine nature into himself and does not penetrate into it; he experiences it as the theme of his own division.

The theme of double love occupies a great place in Dostoevsky's novels. The image of double love is particularly interesting in *The Idiot*. Myshkin loves both Nastasya Filippovna and Aglaya. Myshkin is a pure person; in him there is an angelic nature. He is free from the dark element of voluptuousness. But even his love is sick, divided, hopelessly tragic. For him too the object of love is doubled. And this doubling is merely the collision of two principles within himself. He is powerless to unite either with Aglaya or with Nastasya Filippovna; by his nature he is incapable of marriage, of conjugal love. The image of Aglaya captivates him, and he is ready to be her faithful knight. But while other heroes of Dostoevsky suffer from an excess of voluptuousness, he suffers from its absence. He lacks even healthy sensuality. His love is bloodless and fleshless. But with all the greater force is the other pole of love expressed in him, and before him opens the other abyss of love.

He loves Nastasya Filippovna with pity, with compassion, and his compassion is boundless. There is something that reduces to ashes in this compassion. In his compassion he manifests self-will; he crosses the boundaries of what is permitted. The abyss of compassion swallows and destroys him. He would like to transfer into eternal divine life that lacerated compassion which is generated by the conditions of relative earthly life. He wants to impose upon God his boundless compassion for Nastasya Filippovna. In the name of this compassion he forgets his obligations toward his own personality. In his compassion there is no wholeness of spirit; he is weakened by division, since he also loves Aglaya with a different love.

Dostoevsky shows how in a pure, angel-like being there is revealed a sick love that brings destruction rather than salvation. In Myshkin's love there is no grace-filled striving toward a unified, integral object of love, toward complete union. Such boundless, consuming compassion is only possible toward a being with whom one will never be united. Myshkin's nature is also a Dionysian nature, but it is a distinctive, quiet, Christian Dionysianism. Myshkin constantly abides in a quiet ecstasy, a kind of angelic frenzy. And perhaps all of Myshkin's misfortune lies in the fact that he was too much like an angel and was insufficiently human, not fully human. Therefore the image of Myshkin stands apart from those images of Dostoevsky in which he depicts the fate of the human being. In Alyosha he attempted to give a positive image of a human being to whom nothing human is foreign, who possesses all the passionate nature of man and who overcomes division, who emerges into the light. I do not think this image was particularly successful for Dostoevsky. But one could not stop at the angel-like image of Myshkin, to whom much that is human was foreign, as the way out of the tragedy of the human being.

The tragedy of love in Myshkin is transferred into eternity, and his angelic nature is one of the sources of the perpetuation of this tragedy of love. Dostoevsky endows Myshkin with a remarkable gift of insight. He perceives the fate of all the people around him, perceives the very depths of the women he loves. In him the perceptions of the empirical world draw close to the perceptions of another world. But this gift of insight is Myshkin's only gift in relation to the feminine nature. He is powerless to master this nature and unite with it.

It is remarkable that in Dostoevsky women everywhere arouse either voluptuousness or pity; sometimes the same women arouse these different attitudes in different people. Nastasya Filippovna arouses in Myshkin infinite compassion; in Rogozhin, infinite voluptuousness. Sonya Marmeladova and the mother of the Adolescent arouse pity. Grushenka arouses a voluptuous attitude toward herself. There is voluptuousness in Versilov's attitude toward Katerina Nikolaevna, and he loves his wife with pity; the same voluptuousness exists in Stavrogin's attitude toward Liza, but in a fading and suppressed form. But neither the exclusive power of voluptuousness nor the exclusive power of compassion unites one with the object of love.

The mystery of conjugal love is neither exclusive voluptuousness nor exclusive compassion, although both principles enter into conjugal love. But Dostoevsky does not know this conjugal love—the mystery of the union of two souls into a single soul and two bodies into a single body. Therefore his love is condemned to destruction from the start.

The most remarkable depiction of love given by Dostoevsky appears in *The Adolescent*, in the image of Versilov's love for Katerina Nikolaevna. Versilov's love is bound up with the division of his personality. He too has a doubled love—passionate love for Katerina Nikolaevna and compassionate love for the adolescent's mother, his lawful wife. For him as well, love is not an emergence beyond the bounds of his own "I," not a turning toward his other and union with that other. This love is Versilov's internal reckoning with himself, his own enclosed destiny.

Versilov's personality appears enigmatic to everyone; there is some mystery in his life. In *The Adolescent*, as in *Demons* and many other works, Dostoevsky employs an artistic device whereby the novel's action begins after something very important has already occurred in the heroes' lives, something that determines the subsequent course of events. The crucial event in Versilov's novel took place in the past, abroad, and before our eyes only the consequences of that event unfold. Woman plays an enormous role in Versilov's life. He is a "prophet to women." Yet he is just as incapable of conjugal love as Stavrogin is incapable of it. He is Stavrogin's kinsman—a softened Stavrogin, at a more mature age. Outwardly we already see him calm, strangely calm, like an extinct volcano. But beneath this mask of calm, almost of indifference to everything, frenzied passions lie hidden.

Versilov's suppressed love—finding no outlet, doomed to destruction—heats the entire atmosphere around him to a white heat, giving rise to whirlwinds. Everyone seems to be in a frenzy from Versilov's suppressed passion. This is always the case with Dostoevsky: a person's inner state, even if expressed in nothing outward, is reflected in the surrounding atmosphere. In the realm of the subconscious, those around him are subjected to the powerful influence of the hero's inner, deep-seated life. Only toward the end does Versilov's mad passion break through. He commits a whole series of senseless actions, thereby revealing his secret life.

The meeting and explanation between Versilov and Katerina Nikolaevna at the novel's end belongs among the most remarkable depictions of passionate love. The volcano turned out not to be finally extinct. The fiery lava that constituted the inner substratum of the atmosphere in *The Adolescent* finally broke through. "I will destroy you," Versilov says to Katerina Nikolaevna, revealing the demonic principle in his love. Versilov's love is utterly hopeless and without issue. It will never know the mystery and sacrament of union. In it, the masculine nature remains torn away from the feminine. This love is hopeless not because it receives no answer—no, Katerina Nikolaevna loves Versilov. The hopelessness lies in the enclosure of the masculine nature, the impossibility of emerging toward one's other, in the division. The remarkable personality of Stavrogin definitively disintegrates and perishes from this enclosure and this division.

Dostoevsky deeply investigates the problem of sensuality. Sensuality passes over into debauchery. Debauchery is a phenomenon not of the physical but of the metaphysical order. Self-will engenders division. Division engenders debauchery; in it, wholeness is lost. Wholeness is chastity. Debauchery, however, is fragmentation. In his division, fragmentation, and depravity, a person becomes enclosed within his own "I," loses the capacity for union with another; the human "I" begins to disintegrate. He loves not another but love itself. True love is always love for another; debauchery, however, is love of self. Debauchery is self-assertion. And this self-assertion leads to self-destruction. For what strengthens human personality is emergence toward another, union with another. Debauchery, by contrast, is the profound solitude of a person, the mortal cold of solitude. Debauchery is the temptation of non-being, an inclination toward non-being.

The element of sensuality is a fiery element. But when sensuality passes over into debauchery, the fiery element is extinguished; passion passes into icy cold. This is shown by Dostoevsky with astonishing power. In Svidrigailov is shown the ontological degeneration of human personality, the destruction of personality from unbridled sensuality that has passed into unbridled debauchery. Svidrigailov already belongs to the spectral kingdom of non-being; there is something inhuman about him. But debauchery always begins with self-will, with false self-assertion, with enclosure within oneself and unwillingness to know another.

In Mitya Karamazov's sensuality, the hot element is still preserved; in him there is a hot human heart; in him the Karamazov debauchery does not yet reach that element of cold which is one of the circles of Dante's hell. In Stavrogin, sensuality loses its hot element; its fire is extinguished. An icy, mortal cold sets in. Stavrogin's tragedy is the tragedy of the exhaustion of an extraordinary, exceptionally gifted personality—exhaustion from boundless, infinite strivings that know no limit, no choice, no forming. In his self-will he has lost the capacity for choosing.

And chilling are the words of the extinguished Stavrogin in his letter to Dasha: "I have tried my strength everywhere... In trials for myself and for show, as before throughout my whole life, it proved boundless... But to what to apply this strength—that I have never seen, do not see, and do not see now... I can still, as always before, wish to do a good deed and feel pleasure from it... I have tried great debauchery and exhausted my strength in it; but I do not love debauchery and did not want it... I can never lose my reason and can never believe in an idea to the degree that he does (Kirilov). I cannot even occupy myself with an idea to that degree." The ideal of the Madonna and the ideal of Sodom are equally attractive to him. But this is precisely the loss of freedom through self-will and division, the destruction of personality.

In Stavrogin's fate it is shown that to desire everything without discrimination and without the boundary that forms a person's countenance is the same as desiring nothing, and that boundless strength directed toward nothing is the same as utter powerlessness. From the boundlessness of his objectless eroticism, Stavrogin arrives at complete erotic impotence, at total incapacity to love a woman. Division undermines the powers of personality. Division can only be overcome through choosing, through elective love directed at a definite object—toward God, rejecting the devil; toward the Madonna, rejecting Sodom; toward a concrete woman, rejecting the evil multiplicity of an incalculable number of other women.

Debauchery is the consequence of incapacity for choosing, the result of the loss of freedom and of the center of will, an immersion into non-being as a consequence of powerlessness to win for oneself the kingdom of being. Debauchery is the line of least resistance. Debauchery should be approached not from a moralistic but from an ontological point of view. This is precisely what Dostoevsky does.

The kingdom of Karamazovism is the kingdom of sensuality that has lost its wholeness. Sensuality that preserves wholeness is inwardly justified; it enters into love as its ineradicable element. But divided sensuality is debauchery; in it the Sodom ideal is revealed. In the kingdom of the Karamazovs, human freedom is ruined, and it is restored only to Alyosha through Christ. By his own powers, a person could not escape this element that draws one toward non-being.

In Fyodor Pavlovich Karamazov, the possibility of free choice is definitively lost. He is entirely in the power of the evil multiplicity of the feminine principle in the world. For him there are no longer any "ugly women," no "frights"; for him even Lizaveta Smerdyashchaya is a woman. Here the principle of individuation is definitively abolished; personality is ruined. But debauchery is not a primary principle destructive of personality. It is already a consequence, presupposing deep injuries in the structure of human personality. It is already an expression of personality's disintegration. And this disintegration is the fruit of self-will and self-assertion.

According to Dostoevsky's brilliant dialectic, self-will destroys freedom, and self-assertion destroys personality. For the preservation of freedom, for the preservation of personality, humility is necessary before that which is higher than one's own "I." Personality is bound up with love, but with love directed toward union with one's other. When the element of love is enclosed within the "I," it engenders debauchery and destroys personality.

The yawning abyss of compassion—the other pole of love—does not save personality, does not deliver from the demon of sensuality, for even in compassion a frenzied sensuality may be revealed, and compassion may not be an emergence toward another, a merging with another. In both sensuality and compassion there are eternal elemental principles without which love is impossible. Both passion and pity for the beloved are entirely legitimate and justified. But these elements must be illumined by the vision of the image, the countenance, of one's other in God, by merging in God with one's other. Only this is true love.

Dostoevsky does not reveal to us a positive erotic love. The love of Alyosha and Liza cannot satisfy us. Nor is there in Dostoevsky a cult of the Madonna. But he gives us an enormous amount for investigating the tragic nature of love. Here he has genuine revelations.

Christianity is the religion of love. And Dostoevsky accepted Christianity above all as the religion of love. In the teachings of the Elder Zosima, in the religious reflections scattered throughout various places in his works, one feels the spirit of Johannine Christianity. The Russian Christ in Dostoevsky is above all the herald of infinite love. But just as in the love of man and woman Dostoevsky reveals a tragic contradiction, so too it is revealed to him in the love of person for person.

Dostoevsky had a remarkable thought: that love for human beings and for humanity can be godless love. Not every love for human beings and humanity is Christian love. In the utopia of the future—brilliant in the power of its insight—recounted by Versilov, people cling to one another and love one another because the great idea of God and immortality has vanished.

"I picture to myself, my dear boy," Versilov says to the adolescent, "that the battle is ended and the struggle has subsided. After the curses, the clods of mud and the whistling, calm has come, and people are left alone as they wished: the great former idea has left them; the great source of strength that until then had nourished and warmed them is departing like that majestic, beckoning sun in Claude Lorrain's painting, but it was already as if the last day of humanity. And people suddenly understood that they were left entirely alone, and at once felt a great orphanhood. My dear boy, I have never been able to imagine people as ungrateful and stupid. Orphaned people would at once begin to press closer to one another, more tightly and more lovingly; they would grasp each other's hands, understanding that now only they alone are everything for one another. The great idea of immortality would have vanished and would have to be replaced; and all the great abundance of the former love for Him who was Immortality would be turned by everyone to nature, to the world, to people, to every blade of grass. They would come to love the earth and life irresistibly, and in proportion as they gradually realized their transience and finitude—and with a special, no longer the former love. They would begin to notice and would discover in nature such phenomena and secrets as they had never supposed before, for they would look upon nature with new eyes, with the gaze of a lover upon his beloved. They would wake and hasten to kiss one another, hurrying to love, conscious that their days are short, that this is all that remains to them. They would work for one another, and each would give to all his whole fortune and by this alone would be happy. Every child would know and feel that everyone on earth is like a father and mother to him. 'Let tomorrow be my last day,' each would think, looking at the setting sun, 'but no matter, I shall die, but they will all remain, and after them their children.' And this thought, that they remain, still loving and trembling for one another, would replace the thought of meeting beyond the grave. Oh, they would hasten to love, in order to stifle the great sorrow in their hearts. They would be proud and bold for themselves, but would become timid for one another: each would tremble for the life and happiness of each. They would become tender toward one another and would not be ashamed of it, as now, and would caress one another as children. Meeting, they would look at one another with a deep and meaningful gaze, and in their gazes there would be love and sorrow."

In these astonishing words, Versilov paints a picture of godless love. This is a love opposite to Christian love—not from the Meaning of being, but from the meaninglessness of being; not for the affirmation of eternal life, but for the utilization of the passing moment of life. This is a fantastic utopia. Such love will never exist in godless humanity; in godless humanity there will be what is depicted in *Demons*. What is presented in utopias never actually comes to pass.

But this utopia is very important for revealing Dostoevsky's idea about love. Godless humanity must arrive at cruelty, at the extermination of one another, at the transformation of the human being into a mere means. There is love for the human being in God. It reveals and affirms for eternal life the countenance of every person. Only this is true love, Christian love. True love is bound up with immortality; it is nothing other than the affirmation of immortality, of eternal life. This is a central thought for Dostoevsky. True love is bound up with personality; personality is bound up with immortality. This is true for erotic love and for every other love of person for person.

But there is love for the human being outside of God; it does not know the eternal countenance of a person, for that countenance exists only in God. It is not directed toward eternal, immortal life. This is impersonal, communistic love, in which people cling to one another so that life may be less frightening for those who have lost faith in God and in immortality—that is, in the Meaning of life. This is the ultimate limit of human self-will and self-assertion. In godless love, a person renounces his spiritual nature, his birthright; he betrays his freedom and immortality. Compassion for a person as a trembling, pitiful creature, the plaything of meaningless necessity, is the last refuge of ideal human feelings after every great Idea has been extinguished and the Meaning has been lost. But this is not Christian compassion.

For Christian love, every person is a brother in Christ. Christ's love is the vision of the divine sonship of every person, of the image and likeness of God in every person. A person must first of all love God. This is the first commandment. And after it follows the commandment of love for one's neighbor. It is possible to love a person only because God exists, the one Father. His image and likeness we must love in every person.

To love a person if there is no God means to honor the person as God. And then the image of the man-god lies in wait for a person—the image that must devour the person, transform him into its instrument. Thus love for a person proves impossible if there is no love for God. And Ivan Karamazov says that it is impossible to love one's neighbor. Anti-Christian philanthropy is a false, deceptive philanthropy. The idea of the man-god destroys the human being; only the idea of the God-man affirms the human being for eternity.

Godless, anti-Christian love for human beings and humanity is the central theme of the "Legend of the Grand Inquisitor." We shall return to it. Dostoevsky approached this theme many times—the denial of God in the name of social eudaemonism, in the name of philanthropy, in the name of human happiness in this brief earthly life. And each time there arose in him the consciousness of the necessity of joining love with freedom. The union of love with freedom is given in the image of Christ.

The love of man and woman, the love of person for person, becomes godless love when spiritual freedom is lost, when the countenance disappears, when there is no immortality and eternity in it. True love is the affirmation of eternity.

Chapter VI.
Revolution. Socialism

Dostoevsky is an artist and thinker of the epoch when underground revolution had begun—revolution in the spirit of people, in the spirit of the nation. On the surface, the old order of life still remained. In the era of Alexander III, this way of life attempted one last time to affirm itself in an appearance of seemliness. But inwardly, everything was already in turbulent motion. The ideologists and activists of this movement themselves did not understand the depths of the process that was unfolding. They did not create this process; rather, it created them. They were active in their outward gestures but passive in the state of their spirit, surrendering themselves to the power of elemental forces. Dostoevsky understood better what had begun and where it was leading. With genius-like foresight, he sensed the ideological foundations and character of the coming Russian revolution—and perhaps the world revolution as well. He is a prophet of the Russian Revolution in the most indisputable sense of the word. The Revolution occurred according to Dostoevsky. He revealed its ideological foundations, its inner dialectic, and gave it its image. He grasped the character of the Russian Revolution from the depths of the spirit, from inner processes, rather than from the external events of the empirical reality surrounding him.

The Devils is a novel written not about the present but about what was to come. In Russian reality of the 1860s and 70s, there was as yet no Stavrogin, no Kirillov, no Shatov, no Pyotr Verkhovensky, no Shigalyov. These people appeared among us later, already in the twentieth century, when the soil had deepened and religious currents had begun among us. The Nechaev affair, which served as the occasion for composing the plot of *The Devils*, in its manifest empirical reality bore no resemblance to what is revealed in *The Devils*. Dostoevsky reveals the depths, brings forth ultimate principles; the surface of things does not interest him. The deepest and ultimate principles must be revealed in the future. And Dostoevsky is entirely turned toward that future, which must be born from the turbulent inner movement he had sensed. The very character of his artistic gift may be called prophetic.

His relationship to revolution is extraordinarily antinomian. He is the greatest exposer of the falsehood and untruth of the spirit that acts in revolution; he foresees in the future the growth of the Antichrist's spirit, the spirit of man-godhood. Yet one could not call Dostoevsky a conservative or reactionary in the ordinary, vulgar sense of the word. He was a revolutionary of the spirit in some deeper sense. For him there is no return to that stable, static, psycho-corporeal domestic order and way of life that existed for centuries before the revolution of the spirit began. Dostoevsky is too apocalyptically and eschatologically disposed to imagine such a return, such a restoration of the old, tranquil life. He was one of the first to sense how all movement in the world is accelerating, how everything is heading toward the end. "The end of the world is coming," he jots down in his notebook. One cannot be a conservative in the ordinary sense of the word with such a disposition.

Dostoevsky's enmity toward revolution was not the enmity of a domestic man defending certain interests of the old order of life. It was the enmity of an apocalyptic man who had taken the side of Christ in the final struggle against the Antichrist. But one who is turned toward the Coming Christ and toward the final battle at the end of times is just as much a man of the future, not the past, as one who is turned toward the coming Antichrist and has taken his side in the final struggle. The ordinary struggle between revolution and counter-revolution takes place on the surface. In this struggle, different interests collide—the interests of those who are passing into the past and being pushed out of life clash with the interests of those who are coming to replace them in the first places at the feast of life. Dostoevsky stands outside this struggle for the first places in earthly life. Great people, people of the spirit, have usually stood outside such a struggle and could not be assigned to any camp. Can one say that Carlyle or Nietzsche belonged to the camp of "revolution" or "counter-revolution"? Probably they, like Dostoevsky, would have to be recognized as "counter-revolutionaries" from the point of view of the revolutionary rabble and revolutionary demagogy. But only because every spirit is hostile to what on the surface of life is called "revolutions," because revolution of the spirit fundamentally negates the spirit of revolution. Dostoevsky was such an apocalyptic man of the last times. One cannot approach him with the vulgar and banal criteria of "revolutionary" or "counter-revolutionary" belonging to the old world. For him, revolution was utterly reactionary.

Dostoevsky discovers that the path of freedom, when it passes into self-will, must lead to rebellion and revolution. Revolution is the fateful destiny of man who has fallen away from divine first principles, who has understood his freedom as empty and rebellious self-will. Revolution is determined not by external causes and conditions; it is determined from within. It signifies catastrophic changes in man's most primordial relationship to God, to the world, and to other people. Dostoevsky investigates to the depths the path that draws man toward revolution; he exposes its fateful inner dialectic. This is an anthropological investigation of the limits of human nature, of the paths of human life. What Dostoevsky discovers in the fates of the individual person, he also reveals in the fates of the nation, in the fates of society. The question "Is everything permitted?" stands before both the individual person and all of society. And the same paths that draw an individual person toward crime draw an entire society toward revolution. It is an analogous experience, a similar moment in destiny.

Just as a person who in his self-will has transgressed the boundaries of what is permitted loses his freedom, so too a nation that in its self-will has transgressed the boundaries of what is permitted loses its freedom. Freedom passes over into violence and slavery. Godless freedom destroys itself. This fateful process of the loss of freedom in revolution and its transformation into unheard-of slavery was prophetically foretold by Dostoevsky, and he brilliantly reveals it in all its twists and turns. He did not love "revolution" because it leads to the enslavement of man, to the negation of freedom of spirit. This is his fundamental motif.

Out of love for freedom he rose up ideologically against "revolution," exposing its first principles, which must lead to slavery. Likewise, "revolution" must also lead to the negation of the equality and brotherhood of people, to unheard-of inequalities. Dostoevsky exposes the deceptive character of "revolution." It never achieves what it uses to seduce people. In "revolution," Antichrist replaces Christ. People did not want to unite freely in Christ, and therefore they are forcibly united in Antichrist.

The question of the nature of "revolution" was for Dostoevsky primarily a question about socialism. The problem of socialism was always at the center of Dostoevsky's attention, and to him belong the most profound thoughts about socialism that have ever been expressed. He understood that the question of socialism is a religious question, a question about God and immortality. "Socialism is not merely a labor question or a question of the so-called fourth estate; it is preeminently an atheistic question, a question of the contemporary embodiment of atheism, a question of the Tower of Babel being built without God, not to reach heaven from earth but to bring heaven down to earth." Socialism addresses the age-old question of the worldwide union of people, of the ordering of an earthly kingdom. The religious nature of socialism is especially visible in Russian socialism. The question of Russian socialism is an apocalyptic question, addressed to the all-destroying end of history. Russian revolutionary socialism is never conceived as a relative, transitional state in the social process, as a temporary form of economic and political organization of society. It is always conceived as a final and absolute state, as a resolution of the destinies of humanity, as the coming of the Kingdom of God on earth.

"How do Russian boys operate up to now?" said Ivan Karamazov. "Some of them, that is? Here, for example, is this stinking local tavern—they come together here, settle into a corner. They never knew each other before in their whole lives, and when they leave the tavern, they won't know each other again for forty years. Well then, what will they discuss while they've caught a moment in the tavern? Nothing but world questions: Is there a God? Is there immortality? And those who don't believe in God—well, they start talking about socialism and anarchism, about the remaking of all humanity according to a new plan. So it comes out to the same devil, the same questions, only from the other end."

In this the apocalyptic nature of the "Russian boys" is revealed. With these conversations of "Russian boys" in dirty taverns, Russian socialism and the Russian Revolution began. And Dostoevsky foresaw where these conversations would lead. "Shigalyov looked as though he were expecting the destruction of the world, and not at some indefinite time according to prophecies that might not come true, but quite definitely—the day after tomorrow, in the morning, at exactly twenty-five minutes past ten." All Russian revolutionaries of the maximalist type look the way Shigalyov looked. This is the gaze of an apocalypticist and nihilist who denies the path of history, the labor of culture that rises by degrees. A nihilistic leaven, hostile to the values of culture and to historical sanctities, lies at the foundation of Russian socialism. But in Russian socialism, being the most extreme and ultimate, it will be easier to expose the nature of socialism than in the more moderate and cultured socialism of Europe.

Socialism as an age-old principle, integral socialism that resolves the fate of human society, is not this or that economic organization. Socialism is a phenomenon of the spirit. It claims to speak of the ultimate, not the penultimate. It wants to be a new religion, to answer man's religious needs. Socialism comes to replace not capitalism at all. On the contrary, it stands on the same ground as capitalism; it is flesh of its flesh and blood of its blood. Socialism comes to replace Christianity; it wants to substitute itself for Christianity. It too is permeated with messianic pathos and claims to bring glad tidings of humanity's salvation from all misfortunes and sufferings. And socialism arose on Judaic soil. It is a secularized form of ancient Hebrew chiliasm, the expectation of a sensuous, earthly kingdom and earthly bliss for Israel. It is no accident that Marx was a Jew. He preserved the expectation of the coming Messiah, the reverse of Christ, whom the Jewish people rejected. But for him, the proletariat was the chosen people of God, the messianic nation. He endowed this class with the features of a God-chosen, messianic nation.

Dostoevsky did not know Marx; he did not have before him the theoretically most perfect form of socialism. He knew only French socialism. But with genius-like insight he sensed in socialism that which was later revealed in Marx and in the movement connected with him. Marxist socialism is built in every respect so as to be the antipode of Christianity. Between them there is a similarity of polar opposition. But Marxist socialism, the most conscious form, is not conscious of its own nature to its depths; it does not itself know what spirit it is of, since it remains on the surface. Dostoevsky goes further and deeper in exposing the hidden nature of socialism. He reveals in revolutionary, atheistic socialism the Antichrist principle, the Antichrist spirit. And least of all because he himself stands on the ground of any "bourgeois" foundations and principles. Dostoevsky certainly had a more radical enmity toward the "bourgeois" spirit than the socialists, who are entirely captive to that spirit. Dostoevsky himself was a distinctive Christian, Orthodox socialist, but this Christian socialism is in everything the opposite of revolutionary socialism; it is turned toward the coming City of God, not toward the building of the Tower of Babel. Socialism can only be combated spiritually in the way Dostoevsky combated it. It cannot be defeated on the ground of "bourgeois" interests, because socialism has its own truth in relation to these "bourgeois" interests.

The inner foundation of socialism is disbelief in God, in immortality, and in the freedom of the human spirit. Therefore the religion of socialism accepts all three temptations rejected by Christ in the wilderness. It accepts the temptation to turn stones into bread, the temptation of a social miracle, the temptation of the kingdom of this world. The religion of socialism is not a religion of free sons of God; it renounces man's spiritual birthright; it is a religion of slaves of necessity, children of dust. Since there is no meaning to life and no eternity, all that remains for people is to cling to one another, as in Versilov's utopia, and arrange happiness on earth.

The religion of socialism speaks in the words of the Grand Inquisitor: "All will be happy, all the millions of people." "We shall make them work, but in the hours free from labor we shall arrange their life like a children's game, with children's songs, choruses, and innocent dances. Oh, we shall permit them even sin—they are weak and powerless." "We shall give them the happiness of weak creatures, such as they were created." The religion of socialism says to the religion of Christ: "You pride Yourself on Your elect, but You have only the elect, whereas we shall bring peace to all... With us, all will be happy... We shall convince them that they will only become free when they renounce their freedom."

The religion of heavenly bread is an aristocratic religion. It is the religion of the elect, the religion of "ten thousand great and strong." But the religion of "the remaining millions, as numerous as the sands of the sea, the weak"—that is the religion of earthly bread. This religion will write on its banner: "Feed them, and then ask virtue of them." And the person seduced by the socialist religion betrays his spiritual freedom for the temptation of earthly bread.

The representatives of the religion of socialism "count it as a merit of themselves and their followers that at last they have conquered freedom and have done so in order to make people happy." "Nothing has ever been more unbearable for man and human society than freedom. But do You see these stones in this bare and scorching desert? Turn them into bread, and humanity will run after You like a flock, grateful and obedient, though forever trembling." And the religion of socialism says to Christ: "You rejected the only absolute banner that was offered to You to make all bow down before You indisputably—the banner of earthly bread—and You rejected it in the name of freedom and heavenly bread... I tell You that man has no care more tormenting than to find someone to whom he can hand over as quickly as possible that gift of freedom with which this unfortunate creature is born."

The religion of socialism sets as its primary goal the conquest of freedom, the freedom of the human spirit, which gives rise to the irrationality of life and its incalculable sufferings. It wants to rationalize life without remainder, to subordinate it to collective reason. But for this, it is necessary to put an end to freedom. And one can make people renounce freedom by the temptation of turning stones into bread. Man is unhappy, his fate is tragic, because he is endowed with freedom of spirit. Make man renounce this unhappy freedom, enslave him with the temptations of earthly bread, and it will be possible to arrange the earthly happiness of people.

Already in *Notes from Underground*, the "gentleman with the retrograde and mocking physiognomy" is a representative of the irrational principle in human life that will prevent the ordering of social harmony and social happiness. In him, man's primordial freedom will rise up—a freedom dearer to man than happiness, than daily bread. Dostoevsky makes a discovery of great importance for social philosophy. The suffering of people and the lack of daily bread for many people comes not from man exploiting man, one class exploiting another class, as the religion of socialism teaches, but from the fact that man is born a free being, a free spirit. A free being prefers to suffer and lack daily bread rather than lose freedom of spirit, rather than be enslaved by earthly bread. Freedom of the human spirit presupposes freedom of choice, freedom of good and evil, and consequently also the inevitability of suffering in life, the irrationality of life, the tragedy of life.

Here, as always in Dostoevsky, a mysterious dialectic of ideas is revealed. Freedom of the human spirit is also freedom for evil, not only for good. But freedom for evil leads to self-will and self-assertion; self-will engenders rebellion, revolt against the very source of spiritual freedom. Boundless self-will negates freedom, renounces freedom. Freedom is a burden; the path of freedom is the way of the cross, a path of suffering. And so man, in his feeble rebellion, rises up against the burden of freedom. Freedom passes over into slavery, into coercion. Socialism is the offspring of human self-assertion, human self-will, but it puts an end to human freedom. How can one escape from this antinomy, from this hopeless contradiction? Dostoevsky knows only one way out—Christ. In Christ, freedom becomes grace-filled, united with infinite love; freedom can no longer pass over into its opposite, into evil violence.

Everywhere in Dostoevsky, the utopia of social happiness and social perfection destroys human freedom, demands the limitation of freedom. So it is in Shigalyovism and in the plans of Pyotr Verkhovensky, as in the teaching of the Grand Inquisitor, who under the mask of Catholicism preaches the religion of socialism, the religion of earthly bread, of the social ant-heap. Dostoevsky is a powerful critic of social eudaemonism, an exposer of its perniciousness for freedom.

Dostoevsky held an idea to which he returned many times: the connection between socialism and Catholicism. In Catholicism, in papal theocracy, he saw the same temptation as in socialism. Socialism is merely secularized Catholicism. For this reason, "The Legend of the Grand Inquisitor," to which we shall return in a separate chapter, was written equally against socialism and against Catholicism. I am even inclined to think that it was written more about socialism than about Catholicism. The thoughts of the Grand Inquisitor coincide to a striking degree with the thoughts of P. Verkhovensky, Shigalev, and other representatives of revolutionary socialism in Dostoevsky's work.

Dostoevsky was convinced that the Pope would ultimately go to meet communism, because the papal idea and the socialist idea are one and the same idea of the coercive ordering of an earthly kingdom. Both the religion of Catholicism and the religion of socialism equally deny the freedom of the human conscience. Catholicism accepted the sword of Caesar and was seduced by the earthly kingdom, by earthly power. It was Catholicism that set the peoples of Europe on the path that was bound to lead to socialism.

In *Diary of a Writer*, Dostoevsky says: "France, in its revolutionaries of the Convention, in its atheists, in its socialists, and in its present-day Communards, still is and continues to be in the highest degree a Catholic nation entirely and wholly, completely infected by the Catholic spirit and its letter, proclaiming through the mouths of its most outspoken atheists *Liberté, Égalité, Fraternité—ou la mort*—that is, exactly as the Pope himself would have proclaimed it, if only he had been compelled to proclaim and formulate Catholic *liberté, égalité, fraternité*—in his style, in his spirit, in the true style and spirit of the medieval Pope. French socialism itself today is nothing other than the truest and most unwavering continuation of the Catholic idea, its most complete and final consummation, a fateful consequence that has been working itself out over centuries. For French socialism is nothing other than the coercive unification of humanity—an idea originating from ancient Rome and later preserved in its entirety in Catholicism."

For Dostoevsky, Catholicism was the bearer of the idea of Roman coercive universalism, the coercive worldwide unification of people and the ordering of their earthly life. This Roman idea of coercive universalism also lies at the foundation of socialism. In both, the freedom of the human spirit is denied. And this denial is inevitable when one professes the religion of the earthly kingdom and earthly bread. The French Revolution was for Dostoevsky "a modification and reincarnation of the same ancient Roman formula of worldwide unification." This "formula" was bound to hold sway over the socialist revolution as well, which Dostoevsky foresaw and predicted. In the struggle that was erupting in Europe, Dostoevsky was prepared to side with Protestant Germany in order to defeat Catholicism and socialism, the Roman idea of the coercive union of people.

In Dostoevsky's time, socialism was found predominantly in France; he did not yet know Social Democracy, which developed in Germany, nor did he know Marxism. Therefore many of his judgments have become dated. But he foresaw something very essential. Of course, Dostoevsky was unjust to Catholicism. One cannot equate the great Catholic world, extraordinarily rich and manifold, with the temptations and deviations of the papal theocratic idea: within it there were Saint Francis and great saints and mystics, there was complex religious thought, there was authentic Christian life. Likewise, in Eastern Orthodoxy there were temptations and deviations of the Byzantine Caesarist idea, and in it there was not that freedom of spirit which Dostoevsky preached in Christianity. Yet this analogy between Catholicism and socialism—these two opposite ideas—is striking. In both there is denial of freedom of conscience; in both there is a spirit of extreme orthodoxy and intolerance; in both there is coercion toward good and virtue; in both there is coercive universalism and coercive union of people; in both there is an organization of life that does not permit the free play of human forces.

The socialist state is not a secular state but a confessional state, similar to the Catholic state; it has a dominant confession, and only those who belong to this dominant confession possess the fullness of rights. The socialist state knows a single truth to which it coercively leads people; it does not leave freedom of choice. But the same is true of the Byzantine Orthodox kingdom. Extremes meet. At opposite poles, freedom of spirit is equally denied. And this denial is inevitable when earthly goals are placed above heavenly ones.[1]

Dostoevsky investigates the nature of revolutionary socialism and its inescapable consequences in the phenomenon of Shigalevism. Here triumphs the same principle that the Grand Inquisitor later develops, but without the latter's romantic sorrow, without the peculiar grandeur of his image. If in Catholicism the same principles are revealed as in socialism, they appear in an immeasurably higher form, one aesthetically more attractive. In revolutionary Shigalevism, a flat principle is revealed—an infinite flatness.

Pyotr Verkhovensky formulates to Stavrogin the essence of Shigalevism thus: "To level the mountains is a good idea, not a ridiculous one. There's no need for education—enough of science! Even without science there's material for a thousand years, but first we need to establish obedience... The thirst for education is already an aristocratic thirst. The moment there's family or love, there's already the desire for property. We'll kill the desire; we'll let loose drunkenness, gossip, denunciations; we'll let loose unheard-of debauchery; we'll snuff out every genius in infancy. Everything reduced to a common denominator, complete equality... Only the necessary is necessary—that shall be the motto of the globe henceforth. But convulsion is also needed; we, the rulers, will see to that. Slaves must have rulers. Complete obedience, complete impersonality, but once every thirty years Shigalev lets loose a convulsion, and everyone suddenly begins devouring one another, up to a certain point, solely so that it won't be boring. Boredom is an aristocratic sensation."

"Everyone belongs to all, and all to everyone. All are slaves and equal in slavery... First of all, the level of education, science, and talent is lowered. A high level of science and talent is accessible only to higher abilities—we don't need higher abilities!" But this universal coercive equalization, this triumph of the deadly law of entropy (the increase and even distribution of heat in the universe) transferred to the social sphere, does not mean the triumph of democracy. There will be no democratic freedoms. Democracy has never triumphed in revolutions. On the basis of this universal coercive equalization and depersonalization, a tyrannical minority will rule...

"Starting from unlimited freedom," says Shigalev, "I arrive at unlimited despotism. I will add, however, that apart from my solution of the social formula, there can be no other." Here one feels the fanatical possession by a false idea, which leads to an essential transformation of the human personality, to the loss of the human image. Dostoevsky investigates how the boundless social dreaminess of Russian revolutionaries, of Russian boys, leads to the extermination of being with all its riches, brings it to the limits of non-being. This is very deeply grounded in his work.

Social dreaminess is by no means an innocent thing. Against it one must set sobriety, severe responsibility. This revolutionary dreaminess is a disease of the Russian soul. Dostoevsky exposed it and made a diagnosis and prognosis. Those who in their human self-will and human self-assertion claimed to pity and love man more than God pities and loves him, who rejected God's world, returned their ticket to God, and wanted to create a better world themselves, without suffering and evil—they arrive with fatal inevitability at the kingdom of Shigalevism. Only in this direction can they correct God's work.

The Elder Zosima says: "Truly they have more fantastic imagination than we do. They think to order things justly, but having rejected Christ, they will end by flooding the world with blood, for blood calls for blood, and he who draws the sword shall perish by the sword.

Were it not for Christ's promise, they would exterminate one another down to the last two men on earth." Words of astonishing prophetic power.

Dostoevsky discovered that dishonor and sentimentality are the foundations of Russian revolutionary socialism. "Socialism among us spreads chiefly from sentimentality." But sentimentality is false sensitivity and false compassion. And it often ends in cruelty. Pyotr Verkhovensky says to Stavrogin: "In essence, our teaching is the negation of honor, and by the open right to dishonor it is easiest of all to attract the Russian man." Stavrogin answers him: "The right to dishonor—why, they'll all come running to us, not a single one will remain there!"

P. Verkhovensky also reveals the significance for the cause of revolution of Fedka the Convict and "pure swindlers." "Well, these, perhaps, are good people, sometimes very profitable, but they take a lot of time—they require tireless supervision." Reflecting further on the factors of revolution, P. Verkhovensky says: "The chief force—the cement that binds everything—is shame at having one's own opinion. Now there's a force! And who has worked at this, who is this 'dear fellow' who has labored so that not a single idea of one's own remains in anyone's head? They consider it shameful."

These psychic factors of revolution indicate that at its very sources and foundations, the human personality is denied—its qualitative character, its responsibility, its unconditional significance. Revolutionary morality does not know personality as the foundation of all moral evaluations and judgments. It is an impersonal morality. It denies the moral significance of personality, the moral value of personality's qualities, denies moral autonomy. It permits treating every human personality as a mere means, mere material, permits the application of any means whatsoever for the triumph of the cause of revolution. Therefore revolutionary morality is the negation of morality. Revolution is amoral by its very nature; it places itself beyond good and evil. And external counter-revolution resembles it all too much.

In the name of the dignity of the human personality and its moral value, Dostoevsky rises against revolution and revolutionary morality. In the revolutionary element, the personality is never morally active, never morally accountable. Revolution is possession, demonic frenzy. This possession, this demonic frenzy strikes at the personality, paralyzes its freedom, its moral responsibility, leads to the loss of personality, to its subjection to an impersonal and inhuman element. The actors of revolution do not themselves know what spirits possess them. Their activity is only apparent; in essence they are passive; their spirit is in the power of demons whom they have admitted within themselves.

This thought about the passive character of the actors of revolution, about their mediumistic quality, was developed with regard to the French Revolution by Joseph de Maistre in his brilliant book *Considérations sur la France*. In revolution, the human image is lost. Man is deprived of his freedom; man is a slave of elemental spirits. Man rebels, but he is not autonomous. He is subject to an alien master, one both human and impersonal. This is the secret of revolutions. This explains their inhumanity. A man who possessed his spiritual freedom, his individual-qualitative creative power, could not be in the grip of the revolutionary element. Hence the dishonor, the absence of one's own opinion, the despotism of some and the slavery of others.

By the character of his worldview, Dostoevsky counterposed to revolution the personal principle, the qualitative character and unconditional value of personality. He exposed the anti-Christian lie of faceless and inhuman collectivism, the pseudo-conciliarity of the religion of socialism.

But in revolution not only Shigalevism triumphs, but also Smerdyakovism. Ivan Karamazov and Smerdyakov are two manifestations of Russian nihilism, two forms of Russian rebellion, two sides of one and the same essence. Ivan Karamazov is the exalted, philosophical manifestation of the nihilistic rebellion; Smerdyakov is its low, lackey-like manifestation. Ivan Karamazov on the heights of intellectual life does the same thing that Smerdyakov does in the lowlands of life. Smerdyakov will carry out the atheistic dialectic of Ivan Karamazov. Smerdyakov is Ivan's inner retribution.

In every human mass, in the mass of the people, there are more Smerdyakovs than Ivans. And in revolutions, as mass movements, quantitative movements, there are more Smerdyakovs than Ivans. It is Smerdyakov who draws the practical conclusion that everything is permitted. Ivan commits sin in spirit, in thought; Smerdyakov commits it in deed, having embodied Ivan's idea in life. Ivan commits parricide in thought; Smerdyakov commits parricide physically, in actual fact.

The atheistic revolution inevitably commits parricide; it denies fatherhood, severs the bond between son and father. And it justifies this crime by the fact that the father was a sinful and wicked man. Such a murderous attitude of son toward father is Smerdyakovism. Having committed in deed what Ivan committed in thought, what Ivan permitted in spirit, Smerdyakov asks Ivan: "You yourself kept saying then that everything is permitted, so why are you so troubled now, sir?" The Smerdyakovs of revolution, having realized in deed Ivan's principle that "everything is permitted," have grounds to ask the Ivans of revolution: "So why are you so troubled now, sir?"

Smerdyakov came to hate Ivan, who had taught him atheism and nihilism. In the interrelations of Smerdyakov and Ivan, there is something like a symbolization of the relationship between "the people" and "the intelligentsia" in revolution. This was revealed in the tragedy of the Russian Revolution, and the depth of Dostoevsky's insight was confirmed. The Smerdyakov principle—the lower side of Ivan—is bound to triumph in revolutions. The lackey Smerdyakov will rise up and declare in deed that "everything is permitted." In the hour of mortal danger for our motherland, he will say: "I hate all Russia." Revolution denies not only personality but also connection with the past, with the fathers; it professes a religion of murder, not resurrection. The murder of Shatov is the lawful result of revolution. And that is why Dostoevsky is an opponent of revolution.

Three solutions to the question of world harmony, of paradise, of the final triumph of good are possible: (1) harmony, paradise, life in the good without freedom of choice, without world tragedy, without suffering and creative labor; (2) harmony, paradise, life in the good at the summit of earthly history, purchased at the price of incalculable sufferings and tears of all human generations doomed to death, transformed into a means for the happy ones to come; (3) harmony, paradise, life in the good to which man comes through freedom and suffering, in a plane that will include all who have ever lived and suffered—that is, in the Kingdom of God.

Dostoevsky decisively rejects the first two solutions to the question of world harmony and paradise and accepts only the third solution. Herein lies the complexity of Dostoevsky's ideational dialectic concerning world harmony and progress. It is not always easy to understand whose side Dostoevsky himself is on. What does Dostoevsky himself accept in the remarkable thoughts of the hero of *Notes from Underground* and Ivan Karamazov? What, finally, is his attitude toward the earthly paradise in "The Dream of a Ridiculous Man" and in the picture painted by Versilov?

The life of Dostoevsky's own ideas cannot be understood statically—it is in the highest degree dynamic and antinomian. In him one cannot seek a simple "yes" and "no." In the rebellion of the underground man and Ivan Karamazov against the coming world harmony, against the religion of progress, Dostoevsky sees a positive truth; it is on their side; he himself rebels. In his brilliant dialectic, he reveals the fundamental contradictions of the doctrine of progress. The path of progress draws humanity toward a future harmony, universal happiness, and paradisiacal bliss for those who will climb to its summit. But it brings death to those endless generations who by their labor and their suffering prepared this harmony.

Can one morally accept a harmony purchased at such a price? Does moral and religious conscience reconcile itself to the idea of progress? And in the words of Ivan Karamazov, the voice of Dostoevsky himself sounds, his own passionate idea: "In the final result, I do not accept this world of God's—and even though I know it exists, I do not admit it at all. It is not God that I do not accept; it is His world, the world created by God, that I do not accept and cannot agree to accept. Let me make a reservation: I am convinced, like a babe, that sufferings will be healed and smoothed over, that the whole offensive comedy of human contradictions will disappear like a pitiful mirage, like the vile invention of the feeble and tiny human 'Euclidean mind'; that, finally, at the world finale, at the moment of eternal harmony, something will happen and be revealed so precious that it will suffice for all hearts, for the soothing of all indignation, for the redemption of all human villainy, all the blood that has been shed by them, so that it will be possible not only to forgive but even to justify all that has happened with people—let all this be and come to pass, but I do not accept it and do not want to accept it."

"Surely I have not suffered in order that with myself, with my villainy and my sufferings, I might manure someone's future harmony." "If all must suffer in order to buy eternal harmony with their sufferings, what do children have to do with it, tell me, please? It is completely incomprehensible why they too should have to suffer, and why they should buy harmony with their sufferings. Why did they too end up as material and manure someone's future harmony?" "I absolutely renounce the higher harmony. It is not worth the little tear of even that one tormented child who beat his breast with his little fist and prayed in his stinking little hole with unrequited tears to 'dear God.' It is not worth it, because those tears remained unrequited. They must be requited, otherwise there can be no harmony."

And Ivan Karamazov refuses to be an architect of the building of human destiny if for this it is necessary to torture even one tiny creature. He refuses even the knowledge of good and evil. "Why know this accursed good and evil, when it costs so much?" Ivan Karamazov returns his ticket to God for entrance to the world harmony.

Did Dostoevsky fully share Ivan Karamazov's train of thought? Both yes and no. The dialectic of Ivan Karamazov is the dialectic of the "Euclidean mind"; it is the dialectic of an atheist who has refused to accept the Meaning of world life. Dostoevsky rises above the limitations of the "Euclidean mind," and he believes in God and in the Meaning of the world. But in Ivan Karamazov's rebellion there is a moment of truth being revealed, which is also the truth of Dostoevsky himself.

If there is no God, if there is no Redeemer and redemption, if there is no meaning to the historical process hidden from the "Euclidean mind," then the world must be rejected, then one must refuse the coming harmony, then progress is a monstrous idea. Ivan Karamazov in his rebellion goes further than all the usual heralds of the religion of progress, of the religion of revolutionary socialism. He rejects not only God but the world as well. In this there is a brilliant insight.

Usually atheistic consciousness arrives at world-deification. The world is affirmed with particular force precisely because there is no God, because there is nothing besides "this world." If there is no divine Meaning in the world, then man himself posits this meaning in the coming world harmony. Dostoevsky goes further; he reveals the ultimate limits of rebellion that rejects God and the divine Meaning of the world. The atheism of the "Euclidean mind" must also reject the world, must rise up against the coming world harmony as well, must cast off the last religion—the religion of progress. And at this limit of rebellion, there is a contact with some positive truth. After this, only one path remains: the path to Christ. The limit of rebellion is non-being, the annihilation of the world. Thus the illusions of the revolutionary religion of progress are exposed.

This is why Dostoevsky is halfway together with Ivan Karamazov. Through his dialectic, he leads us to Christ. The world can be accepted, and historical progress with its incalculable sufferings can be justified, if there is a divine Meaning hidden from the "Euclidean mind," if there is a Redeemer, if life in this world is redemption, and if final world harmony is achieved in the Kingdom of God and not in the kingdom of this world.

The path of self-will and rebellion leads to the negation of its own results; it is suicidal. The revolutionary path of self-will leads to the religion of progress and the religion of socialism. But at its limit, it inevitably rejects the religion of progress and the religion of socialism. Rebellion against history must pass into rebellion against the final results of history, against its ultimate goal. In order to justify and accept the future, one must justify and accept the past. The future and the past have one destiny. It is necessary to conquer the evil, fragmented time, to unite the past, present, and future in eternity. Only then can the world process be justified. Only then can one be reconciled to the "little tear of a child."

The world process can be accepted if there is immortality. If there is no immortality, then the world process must be rejected. This was Dostoevsky's fundamental thought. Therefore, the second solution to the question of world harmony proposed by the religion of progress, Dostoevsky radically rejects and rises against. But the first solution is also unacceptable to him. World harmony without freedom, without knowledge of good and evil, not earned through the tragedy of the world process, is worthless. There is no return to the lost paradise. Man must come to world harmony through freedom of choice, through the free overcoming of evil. Coercive world harmony cannot be justified and is not needed; it does not correspond to the dignity of the sons of God. Thus the paradise in "The Dream of a Ridiculous Man" is exposed. Man must accept to the end the suffering path of freedom. And Dostoevsky reveals the ultimate results of this path.

World-deification and man-deification lead to ruin and non-being. And the transition to the God-human path is inevitable. In Christ, human freedom is reconciled with divine harmony. The possibility of a third solution to the question of world harmony is revealed.

For Dostoevsky, the question of world harmony and paradise was resolved through the Church. Dostoevsky had his own theocratic utopia, which he counterposed not only to the utopias of social paradise on earth but also to the utopia of Catholic theocracy. The Church is called to reign in the world. "It is not the Church that is transformed into the state," says Father Paissy. "That is Rome and its dream. That is the third temptation of the devil. On the contrary, the state is transformed into the Church, ascends to the Church, and becomes the Church on earth. This is utterly the opposite of Ultramontanism and Rome, and is only the great destiny of Orthodoxy on earth. From the East shall this star shine forth." "So be it, so be it, even if at the end of the ages."

The Church is not yet the kingdom, the Kingdom of God, as Catholicism teaches following Blessed Augustine. But in the Church the kingdom must be revealed. This will be a new revelation in the Church, toward which Dostoevsky was turned as toward the realization of the prophetic side of Christianity. In the Russian people, as an apocalyptic people, this religious newness must be revealed, but in them also the untruth of atheistic revolution and atheistic socialism will be finally exposed.

In the new Christianity toward which Dostoevsky turns, an extraordinary freedom and brotherhood in Christ must be revealed. Dostoevsky counterposed social love to social hatred. Like all Russian religious thinkers, Dostoevsky was an opponent of "bourgeois" civilization. And he was an enemy of Western Europe insofar as this "bourgeois" civilization was triumphing in it. In his own theocratic utopia, one can find elements of a distinctive Christian anarchism and Christian socialism, so opposed to atheistic anarchism and atheistic socialism. His attitude toward the state was not thought through to the end. His monarchism had an anarchic nature. This brings us to the idea of religious messianism, with which Dostoevsky's positive religious-social ideas are connected—to Russian religious populism.

Chapter VII.
Russia

Dostoevsky was a Russian man and a Russian writer to his very depths. He is inconceivable outside of Russia. Through him one can decipher the Russian soul. And he himself was an enigma of the Russian nature. He united within himself all the contradictions of that nature. Through Dostoevsky, people of the West come to know Russia. But Dostoevsky not only reflected and understood the structure of the Russian soul; he was also a conscious herald of the Russian idea and of Russian national consciousness. In him were reflected all the antinomies and all the ailments of our national self-awareness. Russian humility and Russian self-conceit, Russian universal-humanity and Russian national exclusivity—all can be discovered in Dostoevsky when he steps forward as a preacher of the Russian idea.

When, in his celebrated speech on Pushkin, Dostoevsky addressed the Russian people with the words, "Humble yourself, proud man," the humility to which he called was no simple humility. He considered the Russian people the most humble people in the world. Yet he was proud of this humility. And not infrequently Russian people take pride in their exceptional humility. Dostoevsky considered the Russian people a "God-bearing people," the only "God-bearing people." But such an exclusively messianic consciousness cannot be called a humble consciousness. In it is resurrected the ancient self-perception and self-awareness of the Jewish people.

Dostoevsky's attitude toward Europe was also twofold and contradictory. We shall see that Dostoevsky was a true patriot of Europe, of her great monuments and sacred things; to him belong astonishing words about Europe that no Westernizer ever uttered. In his attitude toward Europe is expressed the universal-humanity of the Russian spirit, the Russian person's capacity to experience everything great that has existed in the world as something native to himself. Yet this same Dostoevsky denied that the peoples of Europe were Christian peoples; he pronounced a death sentence upon Europe. He was a chauvinist. And there is much that is unjust in his judgments about other nationalities—for example, about the French, the Poles, and the Jews.

Russian national self-perception and self-awareness has always been of this sort: either it frenziedly denied everything Russian and renounced the homeland and native soil, or it frenziedly affirmed everything Russian in exclusivity, and then all the other peoples of the world were found to belong to an inferior race. In our national consciousness there has never been measure, never a calm assurance and firmness, without strain and hysteria. And in our greatest genius, Dostoevsky, there is no such firmness either, no fully matured, spiritually masculine national consciousness; one senses in him the sickness of our national spirit.

The structure of the Russian soul is highly distinctive and differs from that of the Western person. In the Russian East opens up an enormous world that can be set over against the entire world of the West, all the peoples of Europe. And perceptive people in the West sense this very well. They are drawn by the enigma of the Russian East. Russia is a vast plain with endless distances. On the face of the Russian land there are no sharply defined forms, no boundaries. In the structure of the Russian land there is no manifold complexity of mountains and valleys, no limits that impart form to each part. The Russian element is spread across the plain; it always recedes into infinity.

And in the geography of the Russian land there is a correspondence with the geography of the Russian soul. The structure of a land, the geography of a people, is always merely a symbolic expression of the structure of that people's soul, merely a geography of the soul. Everything external is always merely an expression of the internal, merely a symbol of spirit. And the flatness of the Russian land, its boundlessness, the infinity of its distances, its unformed elemental character—all this is merely an expression of the flatness and boundlessness of the Russian soul, its infinite distances, its subjection to an unformed national element. All this is but a symbol of the Russian person's nature.

It is not by chance that a people lives in this or that natural setting, on this or that land. There exists here an inner connection. Nature itself, the land itself, is determined by the fundamental orientation of the people's soul. The Russian plains, like the Russian ravines, are symbols of the Russian soul. In the entire structure of the Russian land one senses the difficulty for a person to master this land, to give it form, to subject it to culture. The Russian person is in the power of his nature, in the power of his land, in the power of the element. This means that in the structure of the Russian person's soul, form does not master content; spirit does not master the psycho-corporeal element. In the very structure of the Russian land one feels the difficulty of spiritual self-discipline for the Russian person. The soul spreads out across the endless plain, recedes into infinite distances. Distance, infinity draws the Russian soul. It cannot live within boundaries and forms, within the differentiations of culture; this soul is directed toward the final and the ultimate, because it knows no boundaries and forms of life, encounters no disciplining contours and limits in the structure of its land, in its element.

This is an apocalyptic soul in its fundamental mood and orientation—a soul exceptionally sensitive to mystical and apocalyptic currents. It is not turned into a fortress, like the soul of the European person; it is not armored by religious and cultural discipline. This soul opens itself to all distances, is directed toward the distance of history's end. It easily tears itself away from any soil and is carried off in an elemental whirlwind into infinite distance. It has a propensity for wandering across the endless plains of the Russian land. The lack of form, the weakness of discipline, leads to the Russian person having no real instinct of self-preservation; he easily destroys himself, burns himself up, scatters himself in space. Remarkable words were spoken by Andrei Bely in a wonderful poem dedicated to Russia:

Vanish into space, vanish, Russia, my Russia!

The Russian soul is capable of reaching an ecstasy of ruin. It treasures little, is firmly attached to little. It has no such bond with culture, no such constraint of tradition and heritage, as the Western European soul has. The Russian person experiences a crisis of culture all too easily, without yet having truly known culture. Hence the nihilism characteristic of the Russian person. He easily renounces science and art, the state and economy; he rebels against inherited bonds and rushes toward the kingdom of the unknown, into unknown distances. The Russian soul is capable of radical experiments of which the European soul is incapable—the latter being too formed, too differentiated, too enclosed within limits and boundaries, too bound by the tradition and heritage of its lineage.

Only upon the Russian soul could those spiritual experiments be performed that Dostoevsky performed. Dostoevsky investigated the infinite possibilities of the human soul; the forms and limits of the Western European soul, its cultural bonds and rational hardening, would have been an obstacle to such investigations. This is why Dostoevsky is conceivable only in Russia, and only the Russian soul can be the material upon which he made his discoveries.

Dostoevsky was a distinctive kind of populist; he professed and preached a religious populism. Populism is an original product of the Russian spirit. There is no populism in the West; it is a purely Russian phenomenon. Only in Russia can one encounter these eternal oppositions between "intelligentsia" and "the people," this idealization of "the people" reaching the point of veneration, this search for truth and God in "the people." Populism has always been a sign of weakness in Russia's cultured stratum, of the absence within it of a healthy awareness of its own mission.

Russia took shape as a boundless and dark peasant kingdom headed by a tsar, with an insignificant development of classes, with a small and comparatively weak upper cultural stratum, with a hypertrophied apparatus of the protective state. Such a structure of Russian society, very different from that of European society, led to our upper cultural stratum feeling its helplessness before the popular element—before the dark ocean of the people—feeling the danger of being swallowed up by that ocean. The cultured stratum was supported by tsarist power not in proportion to the people's need for higher culture. Tsarist power, religiously sanctioned in the consciousness of the people, both protected the cultural stratum from the darkness of the people and persecuted it. The cultured stratum felt itself in a vise.

In the nineteenth century, the consciousness of the cultured stratum, which from a certain moment began to call itself the "intelligentsia," became tragic. This consciousness is pathological; there is no healthy strength in it. The upper cultural stratum, which had no firm cultural traditions in Russian history, which felt no organic connection with a differentiated society, with strong classes proud of their glorious historical past, was placed between two mysterious elements of Russian history—the element of tsarist power and the element of popular life. From an instinct of spiritual self-preservation, it began to idealize now one principle, now the other, now both together, seeking in them points of support.

Over the dark abyss of the people, vast as an ocean, the cultured stratum sensed all its helplessness and the dread danger of being swallowed by that abyss. And so the cultured stratum, renamed the "intelligentsia" after the arrival of the raznochintsy, capitulated before the popular element and began to worship the very force that threatened to devour it. "The people" appeared to the "intelligentsia" as a mysterious power, alien and attractive. In the people lies hidden the secret of true life; in them there is some special truth; in them is God, who has been lost by the cultured stratum.

The "intelligentsia" did not feel itself to be an organic stratum of Russian life; it had lost its wholeness, had torn itself away from its roots. Wholeness was preserved in "the people"; "the people" live an organic life; they know some immediate truth of life. The cultured stratum did not have the strength to recognize its own cultural mission before the people, its duty to bring light into the darkness of the popular element. It doubted its own luminosity, did not believe in its own truth, subjected the unconditional value of culture to doubt.

With such an attitude toward culture as was manifested in our cultured stratum, one cannot fulfill a genuine cultural mission. The truth of culture was subjected to religious, moral, and social doubt. Culture was born in unrighteousness, it was purchased at too high a price, it signifies a rupture with popular life, a violation of organic wholeness. Culture is guilt before "the people," a departure from "the people" and a forgetting of "the people." This feeling of guilt pursued the Russian intelligentsia throughout the entire nineteenth century and undermined creative cultural energy.

In the Russian "intelligentsia" there was absolutely no awareness of the unconditional values of culture, no unconditional right to create those values. Cultural values were subjected to moral doubt, held under suspicion. This is very characteristic of Russian populism. Truth is sought not in culture, not in its objective achievements, but in the people, in organic elemental life. Religious life is conceived not as spiritual culture, not as culture of the spirit, but as organic element.

I am giving a characterization of the first principles of Russian populism, independently of its various directions and nuances. In reality, populism in Russia divides first of all into religious and materialistic. But even in materialistic populism, which was a degeneration of our cultured stratum, the same psychology is at work as in religious populism. Among Russian atheistic socialist-populists there are features of resemblance to the populist-Slavophiles: the same idealization of the people, the same suspicion of culture. In our extreme "right" and extreme "left" tendencies there are sometimes striking features of resemblance; the same "Black Hundred" element hostile to culture lies hidden in both. One and the same sickness of our national spirit is revealed at opposite poles. The same undisclosed and undeveloped quality of the personal principle among us, the same lack of a culture of personality, a culture of personal responsibility and personal honor. The same incapacity for spiritual autonomy, the same intolerance, the same search for truth not within oneself but outside oneself.

The absence of chivalry in Russian history had fateful consequences for our moral culture. Russian "collectivism" and Russian "sobornost" were esteemed as a great advantage of the Russian people, elevating them above the peoples of Europe. But in reality this means that personality, that the personal spirit, has not yet sufficiently awakened in the Russian people, that personality is still too submerged in the natural element of popular life. This is why only a populist consciousness could feel truth and God not in personality but in the people.

What, then, is "the people" for the populist consciousness—what is this mysterious force? The very concept of "the people" remains very unclear and confused. "The people" in the dominant forms of populist consciousness was not the nation as an integral organism, which includes all classes, all strata of society, all historical generations—the intelligent and the nobleman just as much as the peasant, the merchant and the townsman just as much as the worker. The word "the people" here has not only this ontological and sole legitimate meaning; it has above all a socio-class meaning. "The people" are primarily the peasants and the workers, the lower classes of society who live by physical labor. Therefore the nobleman, the factory owner or merchant, the scholar, writer, or artist are not "the people," not an organic part of "the people"; they are opposed to "the people" as "bourgeoisie" or as "intelligentsia."

In our "left" revolutionary and materialistic populism, such a socio-class understanding of "the people" finally prevailed. But remarkably, even in religious populism, even in Slavophilism, there is this socio-class understanding of "the people," in sharp contradiction with the organic direction of Slavophile consciousness. For the Slavophile as for Dostoevsky, "the people" are above all the common folk, the peasantry, the muzhiks. For them the cultured stratum has torn itself away from the people and is opposed to "the people" and to popular truth. Truth is in the muzhiks, not in the nobles, not in the intelligentsia. The muzhiks preserve the true faith. The upper cultured stratum is denied the right to feel itself an organic part of the people, to disclose within its own depths the popular element.

If I am a nobleman or a merchant, if I am a scholar or a writer, an engineer or a doctor, then I cannot feel myself to be "the people"; I must perceive "the people" as a mysterious element opposite to me, before which I must bow as before the bearer of a higher truth. An immanent relation to "the people" and to what is "popular" is impossible, and this relation will remain transcendent. "The people" is above all "not-I," opposite to me, that before which I bow, that which contains a "truth" that is not in me, that before which I am guilty. But this is a slavish consciousness; there is no freedom of spirit in it, no awareness of one's own spiritual dignity.

The false "populism" of Dostoevsky stands in contradiction with the remarkable words about the Russian nobility placed in the mouth of Versilov: "I cannot but respect my nobility. Among us there has been created over the centuries a certain higher cultural type, which has never existed anywhere else in the world—the type of universal suffering for all. This is a Russian type, but since it is taken from the highest cultural stratum of the Russian people, it follows that I have the honor of belonging to it. It preserves in itself the future of Russia. There may be only a thousand of us—perhaps more, perhaps less—but all Russia has lived until now only to produce this thousand."

The greatest Russian geniuses, at the summit of their spiritual life and their cultural creativity, could not endure the test of height and mountain freedom of spirit; they took fright at solitude and threw themselves downward, into the lowlands of popular life, and from merging with this element they hoped to acquire the highest truth. Russian remarkable people lack the pathos of mountain ascent. They fear solitude, abandonment, cold; they seek the warmth of collective popular life. In this the Russian genius—Dostoevsky—differs essentially from the European genius—Nietzsche. Both Tolstoy and Dostoevsky cannot endure the height and throw themselves downward; they are drawn by this dark, boundless, mysterious element of the people. In it they hope to find truth more than in mountain ascent.

Such too were the first exponents of our national consciousness—the Slavophiles. They stood at the height of European culture; they were the most cultured of Russian people. They understood that culture can only be national, and in this they resembled people of the West more than our "Westernizers" did. But they capitulated before the muzhik kingdom, fell into its mysterious abyss. They did not find within themselves the strength to defend their own truth, to disclose it in their depths as a national, universally popular truth; they went astray on the path of understanding "the people" as common folk opposed to the cultured stratum, and this had fateful consequences for our national self-awareness.

In our "left," irreligious populism, the fateful fruits of the socio-class understanding of "the people" were reaped. The abyss between "intelligentsia" and "people" was deepened and legitimized. National consciousness became impossible; only populist consciousness proved possible. And yet in Slavophilism were laid the foundations for an organic understanding of "the people" as a nation, as a mystical organism. But the Slavophiles too fell victim to the malady, the sickness of our cultured stratum. The same malady afflicts the consciousness of Dostoevsky. Marxism theoretically decomposed the concept of "the people" into classes and thereby dealt a blow to populist consciousness, but then it itself underwent a populist transformation.

Dostoevsky's populism is a distinctive kind of populism. It is religious populism. But the Slavophiles too professed a religious populism. Koshelev used to say that the Russian people are good only with Orthodoxy, and without Orthodoxy they are worthless. The Slavophiles believed that the Russian people are the most Christian, indeed the only truly Christian people in the world. Yet Dostoevsky's religious faith in the Russian people belongs to another epoch entirely.

The Slavophiles still felt themselves firmly rooted in the soil and still sensed the ground as solid beneath their feet. They were people of settled existence who knew the comforts of everyday life. The good nature of Russian landowners who had grown up in their ancestral nests and remained proprietors of those nests all their lives was still strong in them. Nothing catastrophic, no presentiments of an unknown apocalyptic future can be found in them.

Dostoevsky belongs entirely to an epoch of catastrophic world-perception, an epoch religiously oriented toward the Apocalypse. His messianic national consciousness becomes universal, worldwide, turned toward the fate of the entire world. The Slavophiles were still provincials compared to Dostoevsky. Dostoevsky's relationship to Europe is essentially different from that of the Slavophiles—immeasurably more complex and more intense. His relationship to Russian history also changes. Dostoevsky is no longer inclined to idealize exclusively the pre-Petrine Rus'. He attaches enormous significance to Petersburg, to the Petrine period of Russian history. He is a writer of this period. He is interested in the fate of human beings in Petersburgian, Petrine Russia, in the complex tragic experience of the Russian wanderer who has torn himself away from his native soil during this period. In this he follows Pushkin. The very phantasmal quality of Petersburg, so brilliantly described by him, attracts Dostoevsky. The Muscovite landowner and peasant way of life is utterly foreign to him. He is exclusively occupied with the Russian "intelligentsia" during the Petersburg period of Russian history. He is wholly immersed in presentiments of coming catastrophes. He is a writer of an epoch in which the internal revolution had already begun. Dostoevsky was not a Slavophile in the traditional sense of the word, just as Konstantin Leontiev was not a Slavophile. These are men of a new formation. The Slavophiles lacked this exceptional dynamism of Dostoevsky.

In the *Diary of a Writer* we find a number of negative comments about the Slavophiles, not always even fair ones: "The Slavophiles have a rare capacity for not recognizing their own and for understanding nothing in contemporary reality." Dostoevsky defends the "Westernizers" in contrast to the Slavophiles. "As if there were not in the Westernizers the same sensitivity to Russian spirit and nationality as in the Slavophiles?" "We only wanted to point out a somewhat dreamy element in Slavophilism that sometimes leads it to a complete failure to recognize its own people and to a total disconnection from reality. So that in any case Westernism was still more realistic than Slavophilism, and despite all its mistakes, it still went further—movement remained on its side—while Slavophilism constantly stood in one place and even counted this as a great honor for itself. Westernism boldly posed itself the ultimate question, resolved it painfully, and through self-awareness returned after all to the national soil and acknowledged union with national principles and salvation in the soil. For our part, we state as a fact and firmly believe in the certainty that in the present, almost universal turn to the soil, conscious and unconscious, the influence of the Slavophiles has had too little part, and perhaps no part at all." Dostoevsky values the Westernizers for their experience, for their more complex consciousness, for the dynamism of their will.

He is outraged that the Slavophiles set themselves in lordly fashion outside the agonizing process of life, outside the movement of literature, and looked down on everything from above. For Dostoevsky, "Russian boys"—atheists, socialists, and anarchists—are a phenomenon of the Russian spirit. And our "Westernizing" literature is a phenomenon of the

Russian spirit. He stands for realism, for the tragic realism of life, against the idealism of the Slavophiles. Dostoevsky understood the movement of spirit that was taking place in Russia. In his prophetic consciousness he revealed the nature of this movement and pointed to the terrible limits it would reach. He stood on the ground of spiritual experience, of the necessity of testing the spirit. The Slavophiles, however, in his time, in their second generation, had ceased to understand any movement and feared any experience. These are entirely different attitudes toward life. Dostoevsky's "rootedness in the soil" is deeper than that of the Slavophiles. Dostoevsky sees the Russian soil in the very deepest strata of the earth—those that are exposed even after earthquakes and collapses. This is not a rootedness in everyday existence. This is an ontological rootedness, a recognition of the national spirit in the very depths of being.

Dostoevsky's attitude toward Europe is astonishing. Versílov's words are especially interesting in this regard—words into which Dostoevsky poured his tenderest thoughts about Europe. Many of his thoughts he puts into Versílov's mouth. The Russian is a universal man and the freest man in the world. "They (the Europeans) are not free, but we are free. Only I alone in Europe, with my Russian anguish, was then free… Every Frenchman can serve not only his France but even humanity, solely on the condition that he remain as French as possible—likewise the Englishman and the German. Only the Russian, even in our time—that is, long before the final reckoning is made—has already acquired the ability to become most Russian precisely when he is most European. This is the most essential national distinction we have from everyone, and in this respect we are unlike anyone else. In France I am a Frenchman, with a German I am a German, with an ancient Greek I am a Greek, and by that very fact I am most Russian; by that very fact I am a true Russian and most serve Russia, for I set forth her main idea."

"To a Russian, Europe is as precious as Russia: every stone in her is dear and beloved. Europe was our fatherland too, just as Russia was. Oh, even more so! One cannot love Russia more than I love her, yet I have never reproached myself for the fact that Venice, Rome, Paris, the treasures of their science and art, all their history—are dearer to me than Russia. Oh, these old foreign stones are dear to Russians, these wonders of the old world of God, these fragments of holy miracles; and even this is dearer to us than to the Europeans themselves… Russia alone lives not for herself but for an idea, and the remarkable fact is that for almost a century now Russia has lived decidedly not for herself but for Europe alone." No Slavophile could have spoken such words. This motif is repeated in Ivan Karamazov as well: "I want to travel to Europe; and after all, I know that I shall go only to a cemetery, but to the most precious cemetery—that's the thing! Precious dead lie there; every stone over them speaks of such ardent past life, of such passionate faith in their own achievement, in their own truth, in their own struggle and their own science, that I know in advance I shall fall to the ground and kiss those stones and weep over them—at the same time being convinced with all my heart that all this has long been a cemetery and nothing more."

The same is repeated in the *Diary of a Writer*: "Europe—why, this is a terrible and holy thing, Europe! Oh, do you know, gentlemen, how dear to us, the dreamer-Slavophiles—haters of Europe, according to you—how dear to us is this very Europe, this 'land of holy wonders'? Do you know how dear to us are these 'wonders' and how we love and revere—more than as brothers—the great tribes that inhabit her, and all the great and beautiful things they have accomplished? Do you know how much the fate of this dear and kindred land torments and agitates us, to the point of tears and heartache, how those dark clouds gathering ever more thickly over her horizon frighten us? Never have you, gentlemen, our Europeans and Westernizers, loved Europe as much as we, the dreamer-Slavophiles, according to you her primordial enemies." Neither Slavophiles nor Westernizers spoke this way. Only K. Leontiev, who was neither Slavophile nor Westernizer, could have spoken similar words about Europe's past.

Russian religious thinkers of the type of Dostoevsky and K. Leontiev did not reject the great culture of Western Europe. They revered this culture more than contemporary European people do. They rejected contemporary European civilization, its "bourgeois," philistine spirit; they exposed in it a betrayal of the great traditions and covenants of the European cultural past.

The opposition between Russia and Europe for many Russian writers and dreamers was merely an opposition between two spirits, two types of culture; it was merely a form of spiritual struggle against the tendencies of contemporary civilization that extinguishes the spirit. Slavophilism, Easternism, was a peculiar aberration of consciousness. Two spirits struggle in the world, and the spirit of philistine civilization begins to prevail owing to the betrayal of the Christian foundations of culture. The materialist spirit has gained the upper hand over the religious spirit; attachment to earthly goods closes off heaven. Such is the world tendency of contemporary civilization. It first became clearly manifest among the peoples of Europe. Our "backwardness" saved us. And so the temptation arises to think that this world tendency of contemporary civilization has no power over Russia and the Russian people, that we are of another spirit, that it is merely a phenomenon of the West, of the peoples of Europe. Religious currents of Russian thought and Russian literature became colored with the hue of Slavophilism, of Easternism. This was a protective coloring.

Germany at the beginning of the nineteenth century, in the epoch of the great creative rise of German idealism and the Romantic movement, experienced a similar mood and a similar self-consciousness. The idealist spirit, the Romantic mood, the predominance of higher spiritual interests were affirmed as the German spirit, the German mood, German interests—in contrast to the unspiritual orientation of "the West," of France and England. This was accompanied by an exceptional rise and intensity of German messianic consciousness. But later Germany set out on the path of materialization and betrayed her highest spiritual covenants.

The struggle of two spirits, two types of culture—religious culture and irreligious civilization—has always been immanent to Western Europe itself; it was waged on European soil. The French Romantics, the French Symbolists, the French Catholics of the nineteenth century—Barbey d'Aurevilly, Villiers de l'Isle-Adam, Huysmans, Léon Bloy—with their whole being and their whole suffering life-destiny resisted the dominant spirit of the age, that is, the European and French civilization of the nineteenth century, which wounded them no less than it did the Slavophiles, Dostoevsky, and K. Leontiev. And they turned to the Middle Ages as to their spiritual homeland. The entire phenomenon of Nietzsche, with his passionate dream of a tragic, Dionysian culture, was a passionate and painful protest against the triumphant spirit of European civilization.

This theme is universal, and it cannot be understood as a theme about the opposition of Russia and Europe, East and West. This is a theme about the opposition of two spirits, two types of culture within Europe and within Russia, in the West as in the East. To chosen Russian people, to our greatest and most original thinkers and writers, it was given to feel something more keenly in this theme than Western people, who were more constrained by the character of their cultural history. Even Herzen felt something better here than European people of the 1840s felt. But one could not draw from this the conclusion that in Russia this world tendency of contemporary civilization, this irreligious spirit, would not prevail, that the spirit would not decline among us as well.

Into Russia came the Marxists, and they had success. And in Russia too there is a struggle of two spirits, two types of culture—or more precisely, a struggle of spirit against the extinguishing and weakening of spirit, of genuine culture against civilization. And in Russia too it is possible for not spirit, not culture, to prevail. Spirit and culture I not only bring together but identify, for culture is always spiritual by its nature; only civilization can be unspiritual, while culture is always bound up with sacred tradition, with the cult of ancestors.

Dostoevsky felt better than anyone, more keenly than anyone, the duality of what was coming, the growth within it of the Antichristian spirit. He revealed the movement of this spirit in Russia, in Russia first of all. And K. Leontiev, in the last period of his life, despaired that Russia would yet manifest a new type of flourishing culture opposed to the degenerating European civilization, similar to the flourishing cultures of Europe's past. He reached the point of despair, having seen in Russia the triumph of the worldwide leveling process he hated, and he spoke terrible words: that Russia perhaps faces a single religious mission—the birth from her depths of the Antichrist. Thus in our country the idea of religious populism disintegrated from within, an idea against which the course of Russian history deals terrible blows. And tragic proved the fate of the Russian messianic idea.

"Every great nation must believe, if only it wishes to live long, that in it, and in it alone, is contained the salvation of the world; that it lives in order to stand at the head of nations, to unite them all to itself as one, and to lead them in a harmonious chorus toward the final goal destined for them all." Thus Dostoevsky formulates in the *Diary of a Writer* his need for messianic national consciousness. In such messianic consciousness, national exclusiveness and national particularism are absent from the very beginning. A nation's messianic consciousness is universal, ecumenical consciousness. The messianic nation is called to serve the cause of salvation for all nations, for the entire world. And Dostoevsky sets such a task of universal salvation before the Russian people, the God-bearing nation. Messianism is not nationalism. Messianism lays claim to immeasurably more than nationalism. But in it there is no exclusive national self-assertion.

The Slavophiles were to a significant degree nationalists in their consciousness. They believed that the Russian people manifest the highest type of Christian culture. But they did not claim that the Russian people must save all nations and the entire world, must reveal universal truth. In the all-embracing genius of Pushkin, Dostoevsky discovers the universal-humanity of the Russian national spirit. He is struck in Pushkin by "the capacity for worldwide responsiveness and the most complete reincarnation into the genius of foreign nations—reincarnation almost perfect." "This capacity is entirely a Russian, national capacity, and Pushkin merely shares it with our entire people."

In contrast to the Slavophiles, he says that "our striving toward Europe, even with all its enthusiasms and extremes, was not only legitimate and reasonable in its basis but also national; it coincided completely with the striving of the national spirit itself, and in the end it unquestionably has a higher goal as well." "The Russian soul, the genius of the Russian people, is perhaps more capable than all other nations of containing within itself the idea of universal human union, of brotherly love."

Dostoevsky discovers with brilliant sensitivity that the restless and rebellious Russian wandering, the pilgrimage of our spirit, is a profoundly national phenomenon, a phenomenon of the Russian national spirit. "In Aleko, Pushkin already found and brilliantly marked the unhappy wanderer in his native land, the historical Russian sufferer." The entire creative work of Dostoevsky is devoted to the further fate of this wanderer. He interested Dostoevsky most of all. People rooted in the soil, firmly embedded in the earth, people of solid everyday existence—these did not interest Dostoevsky. "The Russian wanderer absolutely needs universal happiness in order to find peace: he will not be reconciled for anything less."

Thus in Russian wandering, in Russian alienation, the universal-human spirit of the Russian people is revealed. Dostoevsky's thoughts here too are antinomian, and this antinomism is generated by the dynamism of thought that refuses to acknowledge anything static or stable. The Russian wanderer has torn himself away from the national soil. Therein lies his sin and the barrenness of his creative life. But the Russian wanderer, whom Dostoevsky considered a product of Russian aristocracy and contemptuously called "gentilhomme russe et citoyen du monde," is a profoundly Russian phenomenon found only in Russia, one of the manifestations of our national spirit. Such antinomian thoughts about the "Russian wanderer" could not have been contained by the smoother Slavophile thought.

Dostoevsky loved the Russian wanderer and was terribly interested in his fate. He considered the Russian "intelligentsia," which had torn itself away from the "people," a national phenomenon. Understanding this attitude is very important for Dostoevsky's worldview. Therefore Dostoevsky's religious populism was a very complex combination of antinomian thoughts. He called for bowing before "the people's truth," for seeking "the truth of the people and truth in the people." By "the people" he sometimes meant a mystical organism, the soul of the nation as a great and mysterious whole, and sometimes predominantly the "common" folk, the peasants. In this was reflected the usual vagueness and confusion of our populist consciousness.

But one can also understand the task of the Russian wanderer differently. He can in his own depths discover and become conscious of the national element and become national precisely by revealing this depth. For the depth of every Russian person is a national depth. The "national" is not outside me, not in the peasant, but in me, in the deepest stratum of my own being, in which I am no longer an enclosed monad. This will be the only correct relationship to "the people" and "the national"—an immanent relationship. I am not "the people," I am torn away from "the people," insofar as I am on the surface and not in the depths. And to become "the people," I do not need any peasants, any common folk; I need only turn to my own depth. The same is true for ecclesiastical consciousness.

What, then, is "the people's truth" that is revealed in the depths? Dostoevsky did not borrow it from peasants, from the common folk, to whom empirically it is foreign; it was revealed in the depth of his spirit. Dostoevsky himself is "the people"—more the people than all the peasantry of Russia.

"The destiny of the Russian is unquestionably all-European and worldwide. To become a true Russian, to become fully Russian, perhaps means only to become the brother of all people, a universal human being. Oh, all this Slavophilism and Westernism of ours is only one great misunderstanding among us, though historically necessary. For the true Russian, Europe and the fate of the entire great Aryan race are as dear as Russia itself, as the fate of his entire native land—because our fate is universal."

In this understanding of Russian destiny and the Russian idea, Dostoevsky is incomparably closer to Vladimir Solovyov than to the Slavophiles or to later Russian nationalists. But in Dostoevsky's messianic consciousness one can discover the contradictions and dangers of all messianic consciousness.

The messianic idea was brought into the world by the ancient Hebrew people, the chosen people of God, among whom the Messiah was to appear. And no messianism exists except Jewish messianism. Jewish messianism was justified by the coming of Christ. But after the coming of Christ, within the Christian world, the messianic consciousness of a nation is no longer possible. The chosen people of God is all Christian humanity. Nations have their missions, their callings, but this consciousness of mission is not messianic consciousness. Jewish messianism was founded on an exclusive rapprochement and identification of the religious and the national. Messianic consciousness is not nationalistic consciousness—which is always particularistic—but rather universal consciousness. The Jewish people was not one people among peoples; it was the one and only people of God, called to the work of world salvation, to the preparation of the Kingdom of God on earth.

And messianic consciousness within the Christian world always represents a re-Judaization of Christianity, a return to the ancient Hebrew identification of the religious-universal with the national. In the ancient Russian claim that Russia is the Third Rome, there were undoubted elements of Judaism on Christian soil. In even more vivid form, this Judaism can be discovered in Polish messianism. Russian messianic consciousness proceeds from the idea of the Third Rome and passes through the entire nineteenth century, reaching its flowering in the greatest Russian thinkers and writers. The Russian messianic idea reached the twentieth century, and here the tragic fate of this idea was revealed.

Imperial Russia bore little resemblance to the Third Rome; in it, in Dostoevsky's words, "the Church was in paralysis," in humiliating subjection to Caesar. The Russian messianists were turned toward the City that is to come; they did not have their own City. They placed their hope in the appearance in Russia of a new kingdom, the millennial Kingdom of Christ. And then Imperial Russia fell, revolution occurred, the great chain binding the Russian Church to the Russian state was broken. And the Russian people made an experiment in realizing a new kingdom in the world. But instead of the Third Rome, they realized the Third International.

And the consciousness of those who realized the Third International also turned out to be, in its own way, messianic consciousness. They were conscious of themselves as bearing light from the East that was to enlighten the nations of the West languishing in "bourgeois" darkness. Such is the fate of Russian messianic consciousness. It exists not only in the monk Philotheus but also in Bakunin. But this reveals that in the very foundations of messianic consciousness a religious lie has been admitted, a false relationship between the religious and the national. The sin of people-worship lies at the foundation of messianic consciousness, and for this sin an inescapable punishment follows.

The contradictions, temptations, and sins of the Russian messianic idea are embodied in the figure of Shatov. But is Dostoevsky himself entirely free of Shatov? He is, of course, not Shatov—yet he loved Shatov, and something of Shatov lived within him. All of Dostoevsky's heroes are parts of his own soul, moments along his path. Shatov says to Stavrogin: "Do you know who are now the only people on earth capable of bearing God, who will come to renew and save the world in the name of a new god, and to whom alone have been given the keys of life and of the new word?" "Every people is a people only so long as it has its own particular god and excludes all other gods in the world without any reconciliation." This is a return to pagan particularism. But further on, Shatov definitively transforms into a Judaist with universal pretensions. "If a great people does not believe that the truth resides in it alone, if it does not believe that it alone is capable and called to resurrect and save all by its truth, it immediately ceases to be a great people and becomes merely ethnographic material... But there is only one Truth, and therefore only one among the peoples can have the True God, even if the others have their own particular and great gods. The sole people that bears God—is the Russian people."

Then Stavrogin poses to Shatov the fateful question: "Do you yourself believe in God or not?" Shatov stammered in a frenzy: "I believe in Russia, I believe in her Orthodoxy... I believe in the body of Christ... I believe that the new coming will take place in Russia..." "But in God? In God?" Stavrogin insists. "I... I will believe in God."

In this remarkable dialogue, Dostoevsky himself exposes the lie of religious populism, of religious people-worship, exposes the danger of populist messianic consciousness. Many Russians believed in the people before they believed in God; they believed in the people more than in God and wished to come to God through the people. The temptation of people-worship is a Russian temptation. And in Russian consciousness the religious and the national are so intermingled that they are difficult to separate. In Russian Orthodoxy this mixing sometimes reaches the point of identification between the religious and the national. The Russian people believe in a Russian Christ. Christ is a folk God, the God of the Russian peasantry, with Russian features in His image. But this is precisely the pagan deviation in Russian Orthodoxy.

National religious insularity and exclusivity, estrangement from Western Christianity and a sharply negative attitude toward it—especially toward the Catholic world—all this stands in manifest contradiction to the universal spirit of Christianity. Every people, like every individual, refracts and expresses Christianity in its own distinctive way. And the Christianity of the Russian people must be a distinctive Christianity, possessing distinctive and individual features. This in no way contradicts the universal character of Christianity, since Christian all-unity is a concrete, not an abstract, all-unity. But in Russian Christianity there was a danger of the popular element prevailing over the universal Logos, of the feminine principle over the masculine, of the soul over the spirit. This danger is felt even in Dostoevsky himself. Often he preaches a Russian God rather than a universal one. Dostoevsky's intolerance is a Judaistic trait in his religiosity.

The figure of Shatov is remarkable in that it combines the revolutionary and the "Black Hundred" elements, revealing the kinship between these two forces. The Russian revolutionary-maximalist and the Russian "Black Hundreder" are often indistinguishable; the features of similarity between them are striking. And both alike succumb to the temptation of people-worship. The popular element clouds their reason, strikes and disintegrates their personality. Both are possessed. Dostoevsky reveals this because he felt within himself both the revolutionary and the "Black Hundred" principle.

Dostoevsky discovered in the Russian people a dark element, passionate and voluptuous, which our populist writers failed to notice. It is no accident that Khlysty sectarianism was born from the depths of the Russian people—a phenomenon very national, characteristically Russian. In it, Russian Orthodoxy intermixed with primordial Russian paganism, with folk Dionysianism. Russian religiosity, when it assumes ecstatic forms, almost always reveals a Khlysty deviation. The popular element proves stronger than the light of the universal Logos.

In the Russian people, the proper relationship between the masculine and feminine principles, between spirit and soul, has been disrupted. And this is the source of all the maladies of our religious and national consciousness. The dark element of the Russian people is depicted with astonishing power of intuitive penetration in Andrei Bely's novel *The Silver Dove*. Russia is not the West, but neither is it the East. It is the great East-West, the meeting and interaction of Eastern and Western principles. Herein lies Russia's complexity and enigmatic nature.

Dostoevsky possessed the prophetic gift. This gift has been vindicated by history. We felt this acutely when we commemorated the fortieth anniversary of Dostoevsky's death. But it was chiefly the negative rather than the positive prophecies of Dostoevsky about Russia and the Russian people that were vindicated. *Demons* is a prophetic book. This is now clear to everyone. But many of Dostoevsky's positive prophecies, with which *A Writer's Diary* is filled, have not been vindicated. It is painful now to read the pages written about a Russian Constantinople, about the white tsar, about the Russian people as the exclusively and solely Christian people in the world. In one respect Dostoevsky was radically mistaken and proved a poor prophet. He thought that the intelligentsia was infected with atheism and socialism. But he believed that the people would not accept this temptation and would remain faithful to Christ's Truth. This was an aberration of populist consciousness. Dostoevsky's religious populism weakened his prophetic gift. The Russian Revolution refuted Russian religious populism and exposed the illusions and deceptions of populist consciousness.

"The people" betrayed Christianity, while "the intelligentsia" has begun returning to Christianity. What matters most now is to free ourselves definitively from every class-based point of view regarding the religious life of the people. The Slavophiles and Dostoevsky were not entirely free of it. We must turn to the person and seek salvation in the spiritual deepening of personality. And this is more consistent with the fundamental direction of Dostoevsky's own spirit. Slavophilism is coming to an end, and Westernism is coming to an end; Russian populism in any form is no longer possible. We are entering a new dimension of being. And we must develop a new, spiritual, more masculine religious and national consciousness. Dostoevsky gives us infinitely much for the development of this new consciousness. But in him we also study our temptations and sins. On the path to new life, to spiritual rebirth, the Russian people must pass through simple humility and repentance, through severe self-discipline of spirit. Only then will spiritual strength return to the Russian people. Renunciation of messianic pretension must strengthen Russia's national calling. The overcoming of populism must strengthen the person and restore to it the dignity of its spiritual-cultural vocation.

Chapter VIII.
The Grand Inquisitor.
The God-Man and the Man-God

"The Legend of the Grand Inquisitor" is the summit of Dostoevsky's creative work, the crowning achievement of his dialectic of ideas. In it one must seek Dostoevsky's positive religious worldview. In it all the threads converge and the fundamental theme is resolved—the theme of the freedom of the human spirit. It is treated in the Legend in veiled fashion. It is striking that the Legend, which constitutes an unprecedented hymn of praise to Christ, is placed in the mouth of the atheist Ivan Karamazov. The Legend is an enigma. It remains not entirely clear whose side the one telling the Legend is on, whose side the author himself is on. Much is left for human freedom to decipher. But a legend about freedom must be addressed to freedom. Light kindles in darkness. In the soul of the rebellious atheist Ivan Karamazov, a hymn of praise to Christ takes shape. The fate of man inexorably draws him either to the Grand Inquisitor or to Christ. One must choose. There is nothing third. The third is merely a transitional state, a failure to reach the ultimate limits. Self-will leads to the loss and negation of freedom of spirit in the system of the Grand Inquisitor. And freedom can only be found in Christ.

The artistic device to which Dostoevsky resorts is astonishing. Christ remains silent throughout; He stays in the shadows. The positive religious idea finds no expression in words. The truth about freedom is ineffable. Only the idea of coercion is easily expressible. The truth about freedom is revealed only by contrast with the ideas of the Grand Inquisitor; it shines brightly through the Grand Inquisitor's objections against it. This veiled quality of Christ and His Truth produces an especially powerful artistic effect. It is the Grand Inquisitor who argues, who persuades. He has at his disposal powerful logic, a powerful will directed toward the realization of a definite plan. But the unresponsiveness of Christ, His meek silence, convinces and captivates more powerfully than all the force of the Grand Inquisitor's argumentation.

In the Legend, two world principles are set face to face and collide—freedom and coercion, faith in the Meaning of life and disbelief in the Meaning, divine love and godless compassion for people, Christ and antichrist. Dostoevsky takes the idea hostile to Christ in its pure form. He has drawn a lofty image of the Grand Inquisitor. He is "one of those sufferers tormented by great sorrow who love humanity." He is an ascetic; he is free from the desire for base material goods. He is a man of idea. He has a secret. This secret is disbelief in God, disbelief in the Meaning of the world for the sake of which it would be worthwhile for people to suffer. Having lost faith, the Grand Inquisitor felt that the enormous mass of people is unable to bear the burden of freedom revealed by Christ. The path of freedom is a difficult, suffering, tragic path. It demands heroism. It is beyond the strength of such a worthless, pitiful creature as man. The Grand Inquisitor does not believe in God, but neither does he believe in man. These are two sides of one and the same faith. Having lost faith in God, one can no longer believe in man. Christianity demands not only faith in God but also faith in man. Christianity is the religion of God-manhood. The Grand Inquisitor above all rejects the idea of God-manhood, the nearness and union of the divine and human principles in freedom.

Man does not withstand the great testing of his spiritual powers, his spiritual freedom, his calling to a higher life. This testing of his powers was an expression of great respect for man, a recognition of his higher spiritual nature. Much is demanded of man because he is called to something great. But man renounces Christian freedom, the distinction between good and evil. "Why know this damned good and evil when it costs so much?" Man cannot endure his own sufferings and those of others, yet without suffering, freedom is impossible, the knowledge of good and evil is impossible. A dilemma is set before man: freedom or happiness, well-being and the ordering of life; freedom with suffering or happiness without freedom. And the vast majority of people take the second path. The first path is the path of a few chosen ones. Man renounces the great ideas of God, immortality, and freedom, and is seized by a false, godless love for people, a false compassionateness, a thirst for universal earthly order without God.

The Grand Inquisitor rose up against God in the name of man, in the name of the very smallest man—the very man in whom he believes no more than he does in God. And this is especially profound. Those who do not believe that man has as his destiny a higher, divine life are usually the ones who give themselves wholly to the ordering of earthly human welfare. The rebellious, self-limited "Euclidean mind" attempts to construct a world order better than the one created by God. God created a world order full of suffering. He laid upon man the unbearable burden of freedom and responsibility. The "Euclidean mind" will construct a world order in which there will no longer be such suffering and responsibility, but neither will there be freedom. The "Euclidean mind" must inevitably arrive at the system of the Grand Inquisitor—that is, at the creation of an anthill founded on necessity, at the destruction of freedom of spirit.

This theme is already raised in *Notes from Underground*, in *Demons* with Shigalyov and P. Verkhovensky, and is resolved in "The Legend of the Grand Inquisitor." If worldly life has no higher Meaning, if there is no God and no immortality, then there remains only the ordering of earthly humanity according to Shigalyov and the Grand Inquisitor. Rebellion against God must inevitably lead to the annihilation of freedom. Revolution founded on atheism must inevitably lead to unlimited despotism. The same principle underlies the Catholic Inquisition and coercive socialism—the same disbelief in freedom of spirit, in God and man, in the God-Man and God-manhood. The eudaemonistic point of view is inevitably hostile to freedom.

Freedom of the human spirit is incompatible with the happiness of people. Freedom is aristocratic; it exists for the few chosen ones. And the Grand Inquisitor accuses Christ of having, by burdening people with freedom beyond their strength, acted as though He did not love them. Out of love for people, it was necessary to deprive them of freedom. "Instead of taking over men's freedom, Thou didst increase it even more for them. Or didst Thou forget that peace and even death are dearer to man than free choice in the knowledge of good and evil? There is nothing more seductive for man than freedom of conscience, but there is nothing more tormenting either. And instead of firm foundations for setting the conscience of man at rest forever, Thou didst choose everything that was unusual, enigmatic, and indefinite, everything that was beyond the strength of men, and thereby acted as though Thou didst not love them at all." For the happiness of people it is necessary to set their conscience at rest—that is, to take from them freedom of choice. Only a few are able to bear the burden of freedom and follow Him who "desired the free love of man."

The Grand Inquisitor cares for the many, innumerable as the sands of the sea, who cannot bear the testing of freedom. The Grand Inquisitor says that "man seeks not so much God as miracles." In these words is revealed the Grand Inquisitor's low opinion of human nature, his disbelief in man. And he continues to reproach Christ: "Thou didst not come down from the cross... because Thou didst not want to enslave man by a miracle, and didst desire freely given faith, not miraculous faith. Thou didst desire freely given love, and not the servile raptures of a slave before the might that has once and for all terrified him. But here, too, Thou didst judge men too highly, for they are certainly slaves, though created rebels." "In so respecting him, Thou didst act as though Thou hadst ceased to have compassion for him, because Thou didst demand too much of him... If Thou hadst respected him less, Thou wouldst have demanded less of him, and that would have been closer to love, for his burden would have been lighter. He is weak and base."

The Grand Inquisitor is outraged by the aristocratism of Christ's religion. "Thou canst proudly point to these children of freedom, of freely given love, of the free magnificent sacrifice made in Thy name. But remember that they were only some thousands, and those were gods; but what of the rest? And in what way are the rest of the weak people to blame, that they could not endure what the mighty ones could? In what way is the weak soul to blame, that it is unable to contain such terrible gifts? Didst Thou really come only to the chosen and for the chosen?" And so the Grand Inquisitor takes up the defense of weak-willed humanity; in the name of love for people he takes from them the gift of freedom that burdens them with suffering. "Is it that we have not loved humanity, having so humbly acknowledged its helplessness, and with love lightened its burden?" The Grand Inquisitor says to Christ what socialists usually say to Christians: "Freedom and earthly bread enough for everyone are inconceivable together, for never, never will they be able to share among themselves. They will be convinced, too, that they can never be free, because they are feeble, depraved, worthless, and rebellious. Thou didst promise them heavenly bread, but can it compare in the eyes of the weak, ever sinful and ever ignoble human race with earthly bread? And if for the sake of heavenly bread thousands and tens of thousands will follow Thee, what will become of the millions and tens of thousands of millions of creatures who will not be able to neglect earthly bread for the sake of heavenly? Or dost Thou care only for the tens of thousands of the great and strong, while the remaining millions, numerous as the sands of the sea, who are weak but love Thee, must exist only for the sake of the great and strong? No, we care for the weak too." "In the name of that same earthly bread, the spirit of the earth will rise up against Thee and fight with Thee and overcome Thee, and all will follow after him... In place of Thy temple a new building will be raised, once more the terrible Tower of Babel will be raised."

Atheistic socialism always accuses Christianity of not having made people happy, not having given them peace, not having fed them. And atheistic socialism preaches the religion of earthly bread, which millions upon millions will follow, against the religion of heavenly bread, which only the few will follow. But Christianity did not make people happy and did not feed them because it does not recognize coercion over the freedom of the human spirit, over freedom of conscience, because it is addressed to human freedom and awaits from it the fulfillment of Christ's commandments. Christianity is not to blame if humanity did not wish to fulfill it and betrayed it. This is the fault of man, not of the God-Man. For atheistic and materialistic socialism, this tragic problem of freedom does not exist. It awaits its realization and the deliverance of humanity through the coercive material organization of life. It wants to overcome freedom, to extinguish the irrational principle of life in the name of happiness, satiety, and the tranquility of people.

People "will become free when they renounce their freedom." "We shall give them quiet, humble happiness, the happiness of weak creatures such as they were created. Oh, we shall convince them at last not to be proud, for Thou didst raise them up and thereby teach them to be proud... We shall make them work, but in their leisure hours we shall make their life like a child's game, with children's songs, with chorus and innocent dances... Oh, we shall allow them even sin, for they are weak and helpless." The Grand Inquisitor promises to deliver people "from the great anxiety and terrible torments of their present personal and free decision. And all will be happy, all the millions of creatures." "The Grand Inquisitor went away from the proud and returned to the humble for the happiness of these humble ones." And in his own justification he will point to "the thousands of millions of happy babes who knew not sin." But Christ he accuses of pride. This motif recurs in Dostoevsky. In *The Adolescent* it is said of Versilov: "He is a very proud man, and many of the very proud believe in God, especially those who somewhat despise people. The reason is clear: they choose God so as not to bow down before men; to bow down before God is not so humiliating."

Faith in God is a sign of loftiness of spirit; unbelief is a sign of flatness of spirit. Ivan Karamazov understands the dizzying height of the idea of God. "It is a wonder that such a thought—the thought of the necessity of God—could enter the head of such a savage, wicked animal as man, so holy is it, so touching, so wise, and so much does it do honor to man." If there exists a higher nature of man, a calling to a higher goal, then God exists—that is, faith in God exists. But if there is no God, then there is no higher nature of man; then there remains only the social anthill founded on coercion. And in the Legend Dostoevsky unfolds the picture of a social utopia that recurs in Shigalyov and everywhere that man dreams of a coming social harmony.

In the three temptations rejected by Christ in the wilderness, "all subsequent human history was foretold and in them were revealed three images in which all the insoluble historical contradictions of human nature on earth would converge." The temptations were rejected by Christ in the name of freedom of the human spirit. Christ did not want the human spirit to be enslaved by bread, by miracle, and by earthly kingdom. The Grand Inquisitor accepts all three temptations in the name of the happiness and tranquility of people. Having accepted the three temptations, he renounces freedom. First of all, he accepts the temptation of turning stones into bread. "Thou didst reject the only absolute banner that was offered Thee to make all men bow down before Thee indisputably—the banner of earthly bread, and Thou didst reject it in the name of freedom and heavenly bread." The acceptance of the three temptations will constitute the final pacification of man on earth. "Thou wouldst have fulfilled everything man seeks on earth, that is: someone to worship, someone to entrust one's conscience to, and some means of uniting all at last into one indisputable, common, and harmonious anthill, for the craving for universal unity is the third and last torment of men." The system of the Grand Inquisitor resolves all questions of the earthly ordering of people.

The secret of the Grand Inquisitor is that he is not with Christ but with him. "We are not with Thee, but with him—that is our secret." The spirit of the Grand Inquisitor—the spirit that substitutes antichrist for Christ—appears in different guises in history. Catholicism, in its system of papal theocracy that transforms the Church into a state, is for Dostoevsky one of the guises of the spirit of the Grand Inquisitor. The same spirit could be discovered in Byzantine Orthodoxy too, and in every form of Caesarism, and in every form of imperialism. But a state that knows its limits is never an expression of the spirit of the Grand Inquisitor; it does not violate freedom of spirit. Christianity in its historical destiny constantly undergoes the temptation of renouncing freedom of spirit. And there has been nothing harder for Christian humanity than to remain faithful to Christian freedom. Truly there is nothing more tormenting and unbearable for man than freedom. And man finds various ways to renounce freedom, to cast off its burden. This happens not only through renunciation of Christianity; it is accomplished within Christianity itself.

The theory of authority, which has played such a role in the history of Christianity, is a renunciation of the mystery of Christ's freedom, the mystery of the Crucified God. The mystery of Christian freedom is the mystery of Golgotha, the mystery of the Crucifixion. Truth crucified on the cross coerces no one, compels no one. It can only be freely discerned and accepted. Crucified truth is addressed to the freedom of the human spirit. The Crucified One did not come down from the cross, as unbelievers demanded of Him and continue to demand even to our time, because He "desired freely given love, and not the servile raptures of a slave before the might that has once and for all terrified him." Divine truth appeared in the world humiliated, torn, and crucified by the powers of this world, and thereby freedom of spirit was affirmed. Divine truth striking us with its might, triumphing in the world, and by its power taking the souls of men, would not require freedom for its acceptance. Therefore the mystery of Golgotha is the mystery of freedom. The Son of God had to be crucified by the powers of this world in order that freedom of the human spirit might be affirmed.

The act of faith is an act of freedom, the free discernment of the world of invisible things. Christ, as the Son of God sitting at the right hand of the Father, is visible only to the act of free faith. For believing freedom of spirit, the resurrection of the Crucified One in Glory is visible. For the unbeliever, struck and oppressed by the world of visible things, only the shameful execution of the carpenter Jesus is visible, only the defeat and ruin of that which fancied itself divine truth. In this is hidden the whole mystery of Christianity. And every time in Christian history when there were attempts to transform the crucified truth addressed to freedom of spirit into an authoritarian truth coercing the spirit, a betrayal of the fundamental mystery of Christianity was committed.

The idea of authority in religious life is opposed to the mystery of Golgotha, the mystery of the Crucifixion; it wants to turn the Crucifixion into a coercive power of this world. Along this path the Church always assumes the guise of the state; the Church accepts the sword of Caesar. Church organization takes on a juridical character; the life of the Church is subordinated to juridical coercive norms. The Church's dogmatic system takes on a rational character. Christ's truth is subordinated to logically coercive norms. But does this not mean that they want Christ to come down from the cross so that they might believe in Him? In the madness of the cross, in the mystery of crucified truth, there is no juridical or logical persuasiveness and compulsion. The juridicization and rationalization of Christ's truth is the transition from the path of freedom to the path of coercion.

Dostoevsky remains faithful to crucified truth, the religion of Golgotha—that is, the religion of the free. But the historical fate of Christianity is such that this faith sounds like a new word in Christianity. Dostoevsky's Christianity is a new Christianity, although he remains faithful to the original truth of Christianity. In his understanding of Christian freedom, Dostoevsky in a sense goes beyond the bounds of historical Orthodoxy. For a purely Orthodox consciousness, he is of course more acceptable than for a Catholic consciousness, but even conservative Orthodoxy must be frightened by the spiritual revolutionism of Dostoevsky, his boundless freedom of spirit. Like all great geniuses, Dostoevsky stands on the summit. But intermediate religious consciousness unfolds on the plain. The sobornost of religious consciousness is a quality of consciousness; sobornost has nothing in common with quantities, with collectivity; it can exist more fully in a few than in millions. A religious genius may express the quality of sobornost more than a popular collective in the quantitative sense of the word. It is always so. Dostoevsky was alone in his consciousness of Christian freedom; quantity was against him. But in him there was the quality of sobornost. In his understanding of freedom he is akin to Khomyakov, who also rose above official Orthodox consciousness. The Orthodoxy of Khomyakov and Dostoevsky differs from the Orthodoxy of both Metropolitan Philaret and Theophan the Recluse.

The spirit of the Grand Inquisitor can manifest equally on the extreme "right" and the extreme "left." The thoughts of the Grand Inquisitor are repeated by revolutionaries and socialists—by Pyotr Verkhovensky and Shigalev. Shigalev "proposes, as the final resolution of the question, the division of humanity into two unequal parts. One-tenth receives freedom of personality and unlimited power over the remaining nine-tenths. The latter must lose their personality and become something like a herd, and through unlimited submission, achieve through a series of regenerations a primordial innocence, something like a primordial paradise—though they will, of course, still have to work." And Shigalev, like the Grand Inquisitor, was "a fanatic of philanthropy." For the revolutionary Shigalev, as for the Grand Inquisitor, "slaves must be equal; without despotism there has never yet been either freedom or equality, but in the herd there must be equality." Equality is possible only under despotism. And when society strives toward equality, it must inevitably arrive at despotism. The striving for equality, for equal happiness and equal satiety, must lead to the greatest inequality, to the tyrannical dominion of the minority over the majority. Dostoevsky understood and demonstrated this magnificently.

In the "Legend of the Grand Inquisitor," Dostoevsky had socialism in mind even more than Catholicism. The dominion of papal theocracy, with its dangerous deviations, lies entirely in the past. The coming kingdom of the Grand Inquisitor is connected not with Catholicism but with atheistic and materialistic socialism. Socialism accepts the three temptations rejected by Christ in the wilderness; it renounces freedom of spirit in the name of the happiness and contentment of millions of people. It is above all tempted by the transformation of stones into bread. But even if stones could be transformed into bread, it would be at a terrible price—the loss of human spiritual freedom. Socialism accepts the kingdom of this world and worships it. But the kingdom of this world is achieved by that same path—the path of renouncing freedom of spirit. The system of socialism as a religion opposed to Christianity, like the system of the Grand Inquisitor, is founded on disbelief in Truth and Meaning. But if there is no Truth and no Meaning, then only one lofty motive remains: compassion for the human masses, the desire to give them meaningless happiness in the brief moment of earthly life. Here, of course, we are speaking of socialism as a new religion, not as a system of social reforms, not as an economic organization in which there may be its own truth.

The Grand Inquisitor is full of compassion for people; in his own way he is a democrat and socialist. He has been seduced by evil that has assumed the guise of good. Such is the nature of the Antichrist's temptation. The Antichristian principle is not an old, crude, immediately visible evil. It is a new, refined, and seductive evil that always appears in the guise of good. In Antichristian evil there is always a resemblance to Christian good; there always remains the danger of confusion and substitution. The image of good begins to double. The image of Christ ceases to be clearly perceived; it becomes confused with the image of the Antichrist. People appear with doubling thoughts. All of Merezhkovsky's creative work reflects this confusion of the image of Christ and the Antichrist, this constant substitution.

Dostoevsky foresaw the arrival of such a state of the human spirit; he prophetically showed it to us. The Antichrist's temptation appears when a person, in his path, reaches an extreme bifurcation. Then the psychic soil becomes unstable. Then old, familiar criteria are lost and new ones do not arise. Remarkable is the coincidence in the depiction of the Antichristian spirit in the "Legend of the Grand Inquisitor" and in other places in Dostoevsky with Vladimir Solovyov's "Tale of the Antichrist." In Solovyov too, the Antichrist is a philanthropist and socialist; he too accepts all three temptations and wishes to make people happy, to establish an earthly paradise, like Shigalev and the Grand Inquisitor. The same image of the Antichristian spirit appears in the remarkable novel by the English Catholic writer Benson, *Lord of the World*. Benson's novel shows that not all Catholics have been seduced by the spirit of the Grand Inquisitor. In Benson there are the same presentiments and insights as in Dostoevsky and Solovyov.

The unfolding dialectic of Dostoevsky is based on the opposition between the God-man and the man-god, between Christ and the Antichrist. The fate of humanity is realized in the collision of the polar principles of the God-human and the man-godly, of Christ and the Antichrist. The disclosure of the idea of the man-god belongs to Dostoevsky. And this idea reaches particular intensity in the figure of Kirillov. Here we plunge definitively into the atmosphere of the Apocalypse. The ultimate problem of human destiny is posed.

"There will be a new man, happy and proud," says Kirillov, as if in delirium. "He to whom it will be all the same whether he lives or does not live—he will be the new man. He who conquers pain and fear will himself become god. And that God will not exist." "God is the pain of the fear of death. He who conquers pain and fear will himself become God. Then there will be a new life, then a new man, everything new." "Man will become god and will change physically. And the world will change, and deeds will change, and thoughts and all feelings." "He who dares to kill himself is God. Now anyone can make it so that there will be no God and nothing will be." Kirillov believes not in a future eternal life but in an earthly eternal life, when "time suddenly stops and will be eternal." Time "will be extinguished in the mind." The world "will be ended" by the one whose name will be "man-god." "God-man?" Stavrogin asks again. "Man-god," Kirillov replies, "there is a difference."

The social path of man-godhood leads to the system of Shigalev and the Grand Inquisitor. The individual path of man-godhood leads to Kirillov's spiritual experiment. Kirillov wants to be the savior of humanity, to give it immortality. For this purpose he sacrifices himself through an act of self-will; he kills himself. But Kirillov's death is not a death on the cross, not a Golgotha that brings salvation. It is the opposite of Christ's death in every respect. Christ fulfilled the will of the Father. Kirillov fulfills his own will; he declares self-will. Christ is crucified by "this world." Kirillov kills himself. Christ opens eternal life in another world. Kirillov wants to affirm an earthly eternal life. Christ's path lies through Golgotha to the Resurrection, to victory over death. Kirillov's path ends in death and knows no Resurrection. Death triumphs on the path of the man-god. The only immortal man-god was the God-man. Man wants to be the antipode of the God-man, polar to Him and at the same time like Him. In Kirillov, Dostoevsky shows the ultimate limits of man-godhood, the inner destruction of the idea of the man-god. And Kirillov is just as pure, just as ascetic a man as the Grand Inquisitor. The experiment takes place in a completely purified atmosphere. But the entire path of humanity in Dostoevsky, the path of bifurcation, leads to man-godhood. And the inner destructiveness of man-godhood for the image of man is revealed.

Dostoevsky's positive religious ideas, his distinctive understanding of Christianity, must be sought above all in the "Legend of the Grand Inquisitor." In it Dostoevsky is more brilliant, more unique, than in the figure of Zosima and Alyosha, than in the teachings of the *Diary of a Writer*. The veiled image of Christ is akin to Nietzsche's Zarathustra. The same spirit of mountain freedom, the same vertiginous height, the same aristocracy of spirit. This is an original feature in Dostoevsky's understanding of Christ, one that has not yet been pointed out. There has never been such an identification of the image of Christ with freedom of spirit, accessible only to the few. This freedom of spirit is possible only because Christ renounces all power over the world. The will to power deprives both the one who rules and those over whom he rules of freedom. Christ knows only the power of love; this is the only power compatible with freedom. The religion of Christ is the religion of freedom and love, of free love between God and humanity.

How unlike this is to the ways by which Christianity has been attempted in the world! Not only conservative Catholicism but also conservative Orthodoxy must encounter difficulties in recognizing Dostoevsky as their own. In him there were prophetic beginnings; he is turned toward a new revelation within Christianity. He goes beyond the bounds of historical Christianity. The positive ideas that Dostoevsky preached in the *Diary of a Writer* do not express all the depth and novelty of his religious-social ideas. In them he is exoteric; he adapts to the level of average consciousness. One can fully understand his religious ideas only in the light of apocalyptic consciousness. Dostoevsky's Christianity is not historical but apocalyptic Christianity. He poses the apocalyptic theme. And its resolution cannot be squeezed into the framework of historical Christianity.

The figures of Zosima and Alyosha, with whom Dostoevsky connects his positive religious ideas, cannot be considered particularly successful artistically. The figure of Ivan Karamazov is stronger and more convincing, and through his darkness a greater light shines. It is not by chance that Dostoevsky removes Zosima at the very beginning of the novel. He could not have shown him throughout the entire novel. But nevertheless, in Zosima he succeeded in embodying features of his new Christianity. Zosima is not an image of traditional eldership. He does not resemble the Optina elder Ambrose. The Optina elders did not recognize him as their own. Zosima has already traversed the tragic path along which Dostoevsky leads humanity. He understood the Karamazov element in man all too well. He could already respond to the new torment of humanity, to which elders of the traditional type cannot respond. He is already turned toward the joy of resurrection.

An elder of Optina Hermitage probably could not have said: "Brothers, do not be afraid of people's sin; love man even in his sin, for this is already a likeness of divine love and is the summit of love on earth. Love all of God's creation, both the whole and every grain of sand. Love every leaf, every ray of God's light, love the animals, love the plants, love every thing. If you love every thing, you will perceive the mystery of God in things." "Love to fall upon the earth and kiss it. Kiss the earth and love it tirelessly, insatiably; love everyone, love everything, seek this rapture and ecstasy. Water the earth with the tears of your joy and love those tears. Do not be ashamed of this ecstasy; treasure it, for it is a gift of God, a great gift, and it is not given to many, but to the elect."

Elder Ambrose was completely foreign to this ecstatic quality. He did not have this orientation toward the mystical earth and the new acceptance of nature. One might look for traits of similarity here with Saint Francis of Assisi, a religious genius who transcends the bounds of official models of sanctity. But the land of Umbria is very different from Russian land, and different flowers grow upon it. The flower of world sanctity that grew on Umbrian soil has no equal. Zosima is only an expression of Dostoevsky's prophetic presentiments, which do not find fully adequate artistic expression. A new sanctity must appear after humanity has traversed its tragic path. Zosima appears after the underground man, Raskolnikov, Stavrogin, Kirillov, Versilov, after the kingdom of the Karamazovs. But from the depths of the Karamazov kingdom itself, a new man must appear, a new soul must be born.

This birth of a new soul is described in the chapter of *The Brothers Karamazov* titled "Cana of Galilee." This chapter breathes the spirit of a new Johannine Christianity. The light of this Johannine Christianity shone for Alyosha after his soul had been enveloped by the darkness of night. The dazzlingly white truth of the religion of Resurrection appeared before him after he had experienced the immeasurable bitterness of triumphant death and decay. He is summoned to the wedding feast. He no longer sees Elder Zosima in the coffin and no longer smells the seductive odor of decay.

"He, the little dried-up old man with small wrinkles on his face, joyful and quietly laughing, came up to him. There was no coffin anymore, and he was dressed the same as yesterday when he had sat with them, when guests had gathered around him. His face was completely open, his eyes shining. How could this be—so he, too, was at the feast, he too had been invited to the wedding at Cana of Galilee." And the little old man says to him: "We are drinking new wine, the wine of a new, great joy."

And the Resurrection in Alyosha's soul conquered death and decay. He experienced a new birth. "His soul, full of rapture, thirsted for freedom, space, expanse." "The earthly silence seemed to merge with the heavenly; the mystery of the earth touched the mystery of the stars... Alyosha stood, looked, and suddenly, as if cut down, threw himself upon the earth. He did not know why he was embracing it; he could not explain to himself why he so irresistibly longed to kiss it, to kiss all of it; but he kissed it, weeping, sobbing, and watering it with his tears, and ecstatically vowed to love it, to love it forever and ever... But with every moment he felt clearly and almost tangibly how something firm and unshakable, like this vault of heaven, was descending into his soul. Some kind of idea was taking hold of his mind—

and now for his whole life and forever and ever. He had fallen upon the earth a weak youth, and he rose a steadfast fighter for the rest of his life, and he knew and felt this suddenly, at that very moment of his ecstasy."

Thus ends in Dostoevsky the path of human wandering. Having torn himself away from nature, from the earth, man was cast into hell. At the end of his path, man returns to the earth, to natural life, and is reunited with the great cosmic whole. But for a person who has traversed the path of self-will and rebellion, there is no natural return to the earth. Return is possible only through Christ, only through Cana of Galilee. Through Christ, man returns to the mystical earth, to his homeland, to the Eden of divine nature. But this is already a transfigured earth and transfigured nature. The old earth, the old nature, is closed to the person who has known self-will and bifurcation. There is no return to the lost paradise. Man must go toward a new paradise.

The collision of old, dark, ossified, superstitious Christianity with new, white Christianity is depicted in the figure of Father Ferapont, the enemy of Zosima. Ferapont represents degeneration and mortification in Orthodoxy, its plunge into darkness. Zosima represents the regeneration of Orthodoxy, the manifestation of a new spirit in Orthodoxy. The confusion of the Holy Spirit with "holy-spirit" represents the final plunge into darkness of Ferapont's consciousness. He is full of malicious feelings against Zosima. Alyosha accepts the Christianity of Zosima, not the Christianity of Ferapont. Therefore he is of a new spirit.

Zosima says: "For even those who have renounced Christianity and rebel against it are, in their essence, of the same image of Christ, and such they remain." These words, monstrous for the Feraponts, indicate that the image and likeness of God have not perished definitively in Raskolnikov, Stavrogin, Kirillov, or Ivan Karamazov, that for them there is a return to Christ. Through Alyosha they return to Christ—to their spiritual homeland.

Dostoevsky was a profoundly Christian writer. I know of no more Christian writer. And disputes about Dostoevsky's Christianity are usually conducted on the surface, not in the depths. Shatov says to Stavrogin: "Was it not you who told me that if it were mathematically proved to you that the truth is outside Christ, you would rather remain with Christ than with the truth?" These words, belonging to Stavrogin, could have been spoken by Dostoevsky himself and were undoubtedly said by him more than once. Throughout his entire life he bore an exceptional, singular relationship to Christ. And he was among those who would sooner renounce Truth in the name of Christ than renounce Christ. For him there was no Truth outside Christ. His feeling for Christ was very passionate and deeply intimate.

The depth of Dostoevsky's Christianity must be sought above all in his relationship to man and human destiny. Such a relationship to man is possible only for Christian consciousness. But in Dostoevsky it was a creation within Christianity. The relationship to man revealed in Dostoevsky's creative work is deeper than the teachings of Zosima and the *Diary of a Writer*. Here something is revealed that has never before existed in world literature. Dostoevsky drew the ultimate conclusions from Christian anthropocentrism. Religion definitively passes into the spiritual depths of man. Spiritual depth is returned to man. And this is done not in the way Germanic consciousness, Germanic mysticism, and German idealism do it. There, in the spiritual depths, the image of man disappeared, vanished into the Godhead. In Dostoevsky, even in the very last depths, the image of man remains. And this makes him an exceptional Christian. Dostoevsky's Christian metaphysics must be sought above all in the "Legend of the Grand Inquisitor," whose bottomless depth has still not been sufficiently fathomed. The Legend is a true revelation about Christian freedom.

Dostoevsky was the herald of a distinctive Orthodox-Russian theocratic idea, of religious light from the East. In *The Brothers Karamazov* this theocratic ideology is outlined, and individual thoughts about it are scattered throughout various places in the *Diary of a Writer*. To some, this theocratic ideology seems the most essential thing in Dostoevsky's ideas. One can hardly agree with this. In Dostoevsky's theocratic ideology there is nothing especially original, and there is much that contradicts his most fundamental and truly original religious ideas. The theocratic idea is in its essence an Old Testament, Judaic idea, later refracted in the Roman spirit. It is connected with Old Testament God-consciousness. Theocracy cannot help being coercive. Free theocracy (Vladimir Solovyov's expression) is a *contradictio in adjecto*. And all historical theocracies, pre-Christian and Christian, have been coercive; they have always been a displacement of two planes of being, two orders—heavenly and earthly, spiritual and material, ecclesiastical and state.

The idea of theocracy inevitably collides with Christian freedom; it is a renunciation of freedom. And Dostoevsky in the "Legend of the Grand Inquisitor" strikes the final, strongest blows against the false theocratic idea of an earthly paradise as a perversion of the theocratic idea. Christ's freedom is possible only with the renunciation of claims to earthly power. But theocracy inevitably presupposes earthly dominion. In Dostoevsky's own theocratic idea, heterogeneous elements—old and new—are mixed. In it there remains the false, Judaic-Roman claim of the Church to be a kingdom in this world; there remains the fateful idea of Blessed Augustine, which must lead to the kingdom of the Grand Inquisitor.

Connected with this false theocratic idea in Dostoevsky is also a false relationship to the state, an insufficient recognition of the independent significance of the state—not a theocratic state but a secular state, justified religiously from within and not from without, immanently and not transcendently. Theocracy must inevitably pass into coercion, must deny freedom of spirit and freedom of conscience; but in relation to the state, it contains within itself an anarchistic tendency. And this false anarchism, this unwillingness to see the religious meaning of the independent state, was present in Dostoevsky. This is a Russian trait, and here perhaps some Russian disease is manifesting itself.

In Russian apocalyptic disposition is reflected the distinctiveness of our spirit; with it is connected a sensitivity to what is coming. But in Russian apocalypticism there is also something unhealthy, a lack of spiritual courage. The apocalypticism of the Russian people, contrary to Dostoevsky's prophecies, did not protect them from the temptation of Antichristian evil. Not only the "intelligentsia" but also the "people" easily succumbed to the temptation of the three temptations and renounced the primordial freedom of spirit.

Dostoevsky was the spiritual wellspring of religious-apocalyptic currents in Russia. All forms of neo-Christianity are connected with him. He also reveals the new temptations that lie in wait for these apocalyptic currents of Russian thought; he foresees the appearance of refined, difficult-to-recognize evil. But he himself was not always free from these temptations. Yet Dostoevsky's eternal, radiant truth remains the truth he proclaimed about man, about human freedom and human destiny.

Chapter IX.
Dostoevsky and Us

Our spiritual and intellectual history of the nineteenth century is divided by the phenomenon of Dostoevsky. The phenomenon of Dostoevsky signified that new souls had been born in Russia. Between the Slavophiles and idealists of the 1840s and the spiritual currents of the early twentieth century lies a spiritual revolution—the creative work of Dostoevsky. An inner catastrophe separates us from the 1840s. We have departed into other dimensions, still unknown to the people of that more peaceful and happier epoch. We belong not only to a different historical era but to a different spiritual era as well. Our world-perception has become catastrophic. It was Dostoevsky who instilled this in us.

The Kireevskys, Khomyakovs, and Aksakovs—with whom Dostoevsky shared certain common beliefs and ideas, as do we—did not yet know that catastrophic world-perception which later seized even such comparatively calm and stable people as, for example, Prince E. N. Trubetskoy. The people of the 1840s still lived in the rhythm of everyday existence; they still felt solid ground beneath their feet, even in those cases when they professed a dreamy and romantic idealism. In their psychic constitution, no abysses had yet formed. Odoevsky and Stankevich resemble people of the Dostoevsky era as little as do the Slavophiles. For the Slavophiles and Westernizers, hostile to each other and constantly arguing, it was easier to understand one another than it is for people of that era and of the era that opened after Dostoevsky.

One person may believe in God, another may not believe; one may be a patriot of Russia, another a patriot of the West—and yet both may belong to the same psychic formation, may have the same spiritual fabric. After Dostoevsky, in those who have partaken of his spirit, the very fabric of the soul changes. Souls that have lived through Dostoevsky turn toward an unknown and dreadful future; these souls are permeated by apocalyptic currents; in them occurs a transition from the middle of the soul to its periphery, to its poles. These souls pass through a doubling that the people of the 1840s did not yet know—people more harmonious, who knew sorrow and melancholy but had never yet encountered doubles. The devil had not yet appeared to them; they had not yet pondered the problem of the Antichrist.

The people of the 1840s, like the people of the 1860s, did not yet live in an apocalyptic atmosphere; they did not reach the final and ultimate, did not reflect upon the end of all things. The word "apocalyptic" can be taken in a psychological sense as well, and then it should be acceptable even to those who reject its religious-dogmatic meaning. And no one can deny that in Dostoevsky everything is immersed in an apocalyptic atmosphere, if one wishes to characterize that atmosphere accurately. In this atmosphere Dostoevsky expressed a certain fundamental trait of the Russian spirit.

The people of the 1840s were idealistically inclined humanists. And in the Orthodoxy of the Slavophiles one senses a very strong humanistic current. Khomyakov, certainly, in his remarkable conception of the Church, was a Christian humanist. Dostoevsky marks the crisis of humanism—both idealistic and materialistic—and in this he has significance not only for Russia but for the entire world. The relation to the problem of man changes radically. If humanism taught that man is a three-dimensional being, then for Dostoevsky man is already a four-dimensional being. And in this new dimension, irrational principles are revealed that overturn the truths of humanism. New worlds are disclosed within man, and the entire perspective changes.

Humanism did not fathom the full depth of human nature—not only the flat, materialistic humanism, but also the deeper idealistic humanism, even Christian humanism. In humanism there was too much good nature and beautiful soulfulness. The realism of actual life, as Dostoevsky liked to say, the actuality of human nature, is more tragic, contains greater contradictions, than the humanist consciousness imagines. After Dostoevsky one can no longer be idealists in the old sense of the word; one can no longer be "Schillers"—we are fatefully condemned to be tragic realists. This tragic realism is characteristic of the spiritual era that arrives after Dostoevsky. It imposes a heavy responsibility that people of subsequent generations could scarcely bear.

The "accursed questions" have become all too vital, all too real—questions of life and death, of personal destiny and social destiny. Everything has become too serious. And if the literary generation of the early twentieth century, reflecting spiritual searchings and currents, does not appear to stand at the proper spiritual height—if at times one is struck by its lack of moral character—it is precisely because everything has become too serious, too real in the ontological sense of the word. In the 1840s, such severe demands would not have been placed upon writers and thinkers.

When new idealistic and religious currents arose in Russia at the beginning of the twentieth century—currents that broke with the positivism and materialism of the traditional thought of the radical Russian intelligentsia—they placed themselves under the sign of Dostoevsky. V. Rozanov, Merezhkovsky, *The New Path*, the neo-Christians, Bulgakov, the neo-idealists, L. Shestov, A. Bely, V. Ivanov—all are connected with Dostoevsky, all were conceived in his spirit, all resolve the themes he posed. People of the new spirit discovered Dostoevsky for the first time. An enormous new world opened up, closed to previous generations. The era of "Dostoyevshchina" began in Russian thought and Russian literature.

Dostoevsky's influence was mightier and deeper than Tolstoy's, although Tolstoy's influence may be more immediately visible. Tolstoy is far more accessible than Dostoevsky, and it is easier to make him one's teacher than Dostoevsky. He is more of a moralist than Dostoevsky. But the most complex and subtle Russian metaphysical thought flows entirely in the channel carved out by Dostoevsky; it all proceeds from him. One can establish two structures of soul, two types of soul: one favorable for receiving the Tolstoyan spirit, another for receiving the spirit of Dostoevsky. And those who love the Tolstoyan spiritual cast and the Tolstoyan path too much—they have difficulty understanding Dostoevsky. People of the Tolstoyan type often display not merely a lack of understanding of Dostoevsky, but a genuine aversion to him.

Souls to whom Tolstoy's smooth monism and Tolstoyan rationalism are congenial cannot comprehend the tragic contradictions of Dostoevsky. The spirit of Dostoevsky repels them and seems to them un-Christian, even anti-Christian. Tolstoy seems to them the true Christian, faithful to Gospel precepts—the very Tolstoy to whom the idea of redemption was as foreign as to no one else, who was utterly devoid of any intimate feeling for Christ. Dostoevsky, who had an exceptional feeling for Christ, a love for Christ, who was wholly immersed in the mystery of redemption—he seems to them a dark, dreadful, un-Christian writer, one who reveals satanic abysses. Here argument is almost impossible. Here two electing wills collide, two primal sensations of being.

In any case, for creative religious thought Tolstoy was almost barren, while Dostoevsky was extraordinarily fruitful. All these Shatovs, Kirillovs, Pyotr Verkhovenskys, Stavrogins, Ivan Karamazovs—they appeared only in the twentieth century. During Dostoevsky's own time they were not actual reality but foresight and prophecy. In the first, small Russian revolution, and in the second, great Russian Revolution, motifs of Dostoevsky were revealed that had remained covered and unexposed in the 1870s. The religious limits of Russian revolutionism are revealed, the non-political character of Russian revolutionaries. The Russian Revolution has brought Dostoevsky very close to us.

While other great Russian writers have turned out to be writers of the pre-revolutionary era, Dostoevsky must be recognized as a writer of the revolutionary era. He wrote constantly about revolution as a phenomenon of spirit. Dostoevsky was a phenomenon of spirit that prophesied Russia's flight into the abyss. And in him there was an alluring and tempting bottomlessness. With him began the era of "accursed questions," the era of deepened "psychology," the era of underground and rebellious individualism—having split off from any stable way of life—and of its opposite pole, foreseen by him: rebellious, faceless collectivism.

All of this is revealed within the revolutionary currents themselves; in them Shatov and Pyotr Verkhovensky touch, Stavrogin and Kirillov, Ivan Karamazov and Smerdyakov. Dostoevsky saw ideal prototypes. "Psychology" in Dostoevsky never remains on the surface of psycho-physical life. In the narrow and precise sense of the word, Tolstoy was a much better psychologist than Dostoevsky. Dostoevsky is a pneumatologist; his "psychology" always deepens to the life of spirit, not soul—to the encounter with God and the devil.

We long ago entered an era when what interests us is not "psychological" questions, but questions about God and the devil, ultimate questions. And the fate of our public life and our revolution stands under the sign of resolving questions about God and the devil. Dostoevsky not only opens an era of "psychology"—that is a superficial characterization of Dostoevsky—

he leads us out of the hopeless circle of psychologism and directs our consciousness toward ultimate questions. L. Shestov is mistaken in wanting to interpret Dostoevsky exclusively as an underground psychologist. Underground psychology in Dostoevsky is merely a moment on the human being's spiritual path. He does not leave us in the hopeless circle of underground psychology; he leads us out of it.

Dostoevsky is not merely a great artist, an artist-psychologist, and it is not in this that one should seek the distinctiveness of his creative image. Dostoevsky is a great thinker. This I have endeavored to show throughout my entire book. He is the greatest Russian metaphysician. All our metaphysical ideas come from Dostoevsky. He lives in an atmosphere of passionate, fiery ideas. He infects us with these ideas, draws us into their circle. Dostoevsky's ideas are spiritual daily bread. Without them one cannot live. One cannot live without resolving the question of God and the devil, of immortality, of freedom, of evil, of the fate of man and humanity. This is not a luxury—it is essential. If there is no immortality, then life is not worth living. Dostoevsky's ideas are not abstract but concrete ideas. In him, ideas live. Dostoevsky's metaphysics is not abstract but concrete metaphysics. Dostoevsky taught us this concrete, vitally essential character of ideas. We are Dostoevsky's spiritual children. We would like to pose and resolve "metaphysical" questions in the spirit in which Dostoevsky posed and resolved them.

Dostoevsky's "metaphysics" is closer to us than the "metaphysics" of Vl. Solovyov. And perhaps the only sense in which "metaphysics" can be preserved is the sense it has in Dostoevsky. Vl. Solovyov too abstractly refuted abstract metaphysics; he does not attain true concreteness. He was close to Dostoevsky, touched him intimately in certain ways—perhaps most of all in the "Tale of the Antichrist"—but he is a parallel phenomenon; he was not conceived from Dostoevsky's spirit.

V. Rozanov was born in Dostoevsky's creative imagination—perhaps the most remarkable Russian writer of recent decades. Even Rozanov's astonishing style derives from the style in which certain characters of Dostoevsky speak. Rozanov had the same concreteness, the same vital urgency of metaphysics, as Dostoevsky. He resolved Dostoevsky's themes. But the phenomenon of Rozanov also speaks of the dangers contained in Dostoevsky's spirit. Through Rozanov's lips sometimes philosophized Fyodor Pavlovich Karamazov himself, who rises to a brilliant pathos. Rozanov's utter lack of any self-discipline of spirit indicates that Dostoevsky's influence can also be enervating.

Merezhkovsky's ideology likewise was born from Dostoevsky's spirit; it is already contained in "Cana of Galilee" and in Dostoevsky's thoughts about the God-man and the man-god. But Dostoevsky did not help Merezhkovsky find a criterion for distinguishing Christ from the Antichrist. He remained in doubting thoughts. And this raises the question: can Dostoevsky be a teacher?

Dostoevsky teaches us much; he reveals much to us. We accept Dostoevsky's spiritual inheritance. But he is not a teacher of life in the strict sense of the word. One cannot walk the path of Dostoevsky; one cannot live according to Dostoevsky. It is difficult to extract from him instruction for the path of life. "Dostoyevshchina" conceals within itself, for Russian people, not only great spiritual treasures but also great spiritual dangers. In the Russian soul there is a thirst for self-immolation, a danger of intoxication with destruction. The instinct of spiritual self-preservation is weak in it. One cannot, after all, summon people to tragedy, preach tragedy as a path; one cannot teach the experience of passing through doubling and darkness.

The tragedy of man revealed to us by Dostoevsky can be lived through, and one can be enriched by this experience, but one cannot teach the experience of this tragedy as a life path. The ecstatic, Dionysian element that gives birth to tragedy must be accepted as a primary given, as a primordial foundation of being, as the atmosphere in which our human destiny is accomplished. But one cannot summon people to the Dionysian element; one cannot give it a normative character. Dostoevsky is very difficult and dangerous to interpret normatively. I spoke of this already when I spoke of the problem of evil in Dostoevsky. It is extremely important to establish the proper relation to Dostoevsky.

Dostoevsky's creative work speaks not only of the fact that the greatest spiritual possibilities are contained within the Russian people, but also of the fact that this people is spiritually sick. For this people, spiritually extraordinarily gifted, it is very difficult to discipline its spirit—more difficult than for the peoples of the West. Dostoevsky does not indicate paths of self-discipline of spirit, paths of giving form to the elemental soul, of mastering with masculine spirit the feminine national soul.

Russians lack character; this must be acknowledged as our national defect. The cultivation of moral character, the cultivation of spiritual masculinity—this is our chief life task. Does Dostoevsky help in this work? Does Dostoevsky help us cultivate true autonomy of spirit, liberate ourselves from every slavery? I have tried to show that the pathos of freedom was Dostoevsky's true pathos. But he did not teach how to acquire freedom of spirit, moral and spiritual autonomy, how to liberate oneself and one's people from the power of lower elements. He was not a teacher of freedom, although he taught about freedom as the primordial foundation of life. For him, Dionysian tragedy, doubling, and the abyss seem to remain the only path for man. The path to light lies through darkness. Dostoevsky's greatness lay in showing how light kindles in the darkness. But the Russian soul is inclined to plunge into the element of darkness and remain in it as long as possible. Difficult for it is the exit from this elemental darkness; difficult is mastering one's passionate elementality.

Russians possess both an exceptional sense of personality and personal destiny, and also an inability to protect their personality from being torn apart by Dionysian passions, to affirm the form of personality. In Dostoevsky, great revelations of the Russian spirit and the world spirit were accomplished. But he does not express that masculine maturity of spirit when spirit masters the chaotic elemental soul, disciplines it, and subordinates it to a higher goal. In Russia, spirit still floats in elemental soulfulness. And this is reflected in Dostoevsky as well.

Even after the greatest manifestation of our national spirit—Dostoevsky—we still do not have a healthy and mature national self-consciousness. What Fichte and people of his spirit accomplished for the German people has still not been accomplished among us. This was fatefully reflected in the course of the Russian Revolution. There was a fateful duality in Dostoevsky. On the one hand, he attributed exceptional significance to the principle of personality; he was a fanatic of the personal principle, and this was his strongest side. On the other hand, the principle of sobornost and collectivity played a great role in him. Dostoevsky's religious populism was a temptation of collectivism, paralyzing the principle of personal responsibility, of personal spiritual discipline.

The idea of religious sobornost among Russians has not infrequently been a false idealization of the Russian people, an idealization of the popular collective as the bearer of spirit. But the Russian people most of all needs the idea of personal responsibility, the idea of self-discipline, personal spiritual autonomy. Only a spiritual reform in this direction can heal the Russian people. Dostoevsky, with only one half of himself, is turned toward this task and helps its realization; with the other half he tempts us with Russian populism and Russian collectivism—that is, he hinders the realization of this task.

In Dostoevsky's creative image, the Russian aversion to middle culture found its expression. Dostoevsky himself was a great phenomenon of Russian culture, its very summit. Yet at the same time, he marked a world crisis of culture. All the currents that were born from the spirit of Dostoevsky find themselves in a crisis of culture, in dissatisfaction with the ultimate achievements of culture. This crisis and this dissatisfaction were bound to be felt with particular acuteness precisely at the heights of culture.

Culture, with all its great values, is a middle ground; in it there is no end, no limit to achievements. And culture does not attain or realize genuine being. It is not ontological; it is symbolic. The crisis of culture is a crisis of the symbolism of culture, which reaches its greatest intensity precisely among the Symbolists. One might venture a paradox: Symbolism is a thirst for the overcoming of symbolism, the transformation of symbolic culture into ontological culture, in which what would be attainable would be not symbols of ultimate reality but ultimate reality itself. Those "realists" of culture who naively remain within the symbolism of culture—unaware of this symbolism, maintaining confidence in the realistic character of all cultural achievements—are not Symbolists at all but opponents of symbolism.

The crisis of culture also signifies a thirst for escape from the middle toward some resolving end. In the crisis of culture there is an apocalyptic striving. It is present in Nietzsche, and it is present to the highest degree in Dostoevsky. But this apocalyptic disposition, this striving toward the end, this suspicious and hostile attitude toward all middle culture—these are characteristically Russian traits. And in these traits of the Russian spiritual constitution we must seek both the sources of our spiritual distinctiveness and the sources of our spiritual maladies.

The rejection of middle culture is a dangerous trait in Russian people; it is a nihilistic trait. When a crisis of culture occurs at such world summits as Dostoevsky, this has an entirely different meaning than when the same crisis occurs among Russian people who do not yet possess genuine culture and who remain in a pre-cultural or semi-cultural state. While in people of the highest and most refined culture Dostoevsky awakens ontological consciousness and a thirst for the transition from the creation of symbolic cultural values to the creation of genuine being, in Russians of little culture he can paralyze the taste for culture and reinforce a nihilistic attitude toward it.

Apocalypticism and nihilism among us always touch upon one another in a strange way. They ought to be more clearly and distinctly separated. The Russian readily strips off all cultural garments in order to reveal genuine being in its natural state. But genuine being does not thereby appear, while cultural values are subjected to devastation. We especially need the consciousness that culture is a path to genuine being, that the most divine life is the highest culture of the spirit.

Tolstoy's influence in relation to culture was pernicious for Russians. Dostoevsky's influence was ambivalent. Such is the fate of great Russian writers. Yet one must still remember that Dostoevsky represented a crisis of culture, but he was not, like Tolstoy, an enemy of culture. Dostoevsky's apocalyptic striving was combined with a recognition of history and of historical sanctities and values, of historical continuity. And in this we must especially feel ourselves to be heirs of Dostoevsky's spirit.

But if Dostoevsky cannot be a teacher of spiritual discipline and the spiritual path, if "Dostoyevshchina"—as our psychologism—must be overcome in us, he nevertheless remains a teacher in one respect: through Christ he teaches us to discover light in darkness, to discover the image and likeness of God in even the most fallen human being; he teaches a love for humanity that is bound up with respect for human freedom. Dostoevsky leads us through darkness, but darkness does not have the last word in his work. Dostoevsky's creative work leaves anything but an impression of gloomy and hopeless pessimism. In his work, darkness itself is light-bearing. The light of Christ conquers the world, illuminates every darkness. Dostoevsky's Christianity itself is not a gloomy Christianity; it is a white, Johannine Christianity.

It is precisely Dostoevsky who gives much for the Christianity of the future, for the triumph of the eternal Gospel, the religion of freedom and love. Much has died in Christianity, and within it cadaverous poisons have been produced that contaminate the spiritual sources of life. Much in Christianity now resembles not a living organism but a mineral. Ossification has set in. With dead lips we pronounce dead words from which the spirit has departed. *The Spirit blows where it will.* But it does not wish to blow in religiously deadened and ossified souls. Souls must be melted; they must undergo a second baptism by fire so that the spirit may begin to blow in them once more.

The victory of the Antichrist's spirit in the world, the loss of faith, the growth of materialism—all these are already secondary results and consequences of that deadening and ossification which occurs within Christianity itself, within religious life itself. Christianity transformed into dead scholasticism, into the profession of soulless, abstract forms, subjected to clerical degeneration—such Christianity cannot be a regenerating force. Within Christianity itself a rebirth and renewal of the spirit must occur. Christianity must become the religion of the new times that are approaching, if it is indeed the eternal religion. A creative movement must begin within it. Such a movement has not occurred for a long time. Dostoevsky melts ossified souls, leads them through baptism by fire. And he clears the ground for a creative rebirth of the spirit, for a religious movement in which will be revealed a new and eternal, living Christianity.

Dostoevsky deserves the title of religious reformer more than L. Tolstoy. Tolstoy demolished Christian sanctities and values and attempted to invent his own religion. And if his merits can be acknowledged, they are negative and critical merits. Dostoevsky does not invent a new religion; he remains faithful to the eternal Truth, to the eternal tradition of Christianity. But within Christianity he awakens a new spirit, a creative movement that destroys and annihilates nothing. He is even prepared to accept all the old formulas. But he infuses a new spirit into them. He is turned toward the future, in an epoch when Christianity lives too exclusively in the past. He recalls the Apocalypse, which had remained a dead letter in historical Christianity. Dostoevsky's creative work is fruitful in the highest degree for Christian renewal. It is a prophetic phenomenon and points toward great spiritual possibilities. But upon this great creative work is imprinted all the duality of the Russian character; in it are given both the great Russian possibilities and the great Russian dangers. And we must work spiritually upon Dostoevsky's legacy, inwardly purify and bring to consciousness the experience he revealed.

Now Western Europe, entering into the rhythm of a catastrophic process, turns to Dostoevsky and is more capable of understanding him. By the will of fate, Western Europe is emerging from the state of bourgeois self-satisfaction in which, prior to the catastrophe of the World War, it had apparently hoped to remain forever. European society for a long time lingered on the periphery of being and contented itself with external existence. It wanted to establish itself forever on the surface of the earth. But there too, in "bourgeois" Europe, comfortably settled as it was, volcanic ground is being revealed. And spiritual depth will inevitably be disclosed among the peoples of Europe. Everywhere a movement from the surface into the depths must occur, although it is preceded by such movements to the surface, outward, as wars and revolutions.

And so, in catastrophes and upheavals, having sensed the call of spiritual depth, the peoples of Western Europe will approach with greater understanding and greater inner need that Russian and world genius who was a discoverer of the spiritual depths of the human being and who foresaw the inevitability of catastrophes in the world. Dostoevsky is that supreme value by which the Russian people will justify its existence in the world, that to which it can point at the Last Judgment of the nations.

www.ingramcontent.com/pod-product-compliance
Lightning Source LLC
Chambersburg PA
CBHW080604170426
43196CB00017B/2901